Pattern + Palette³
SOURCEBOOK

ROCKPORT

First published in the United States of America by
Rockport Publishers, a member of
Quayside Publishing Group
100 Cummings Center
Suite 406-L
Beverly, Massachusetts 01915-6101
Telephone: (978) 282-9590
Fax: (978) 283-2742
www.rockpub.com

ISBN-13: 978-1-59253-494-4
ISBN-10: 1-59253-494-5

10 9 8 7 6 5 4 3 2 1

Series Design: Anvil Graphic Design, Inc.
Cover Design: Mattie Reposa
Layout and Production: Janice Petrie

Printed in Singapore

Pattern + Palette³

SOURCEBOOK

A Complete Guide to Choosing the
Perfect Color and Pattern in Design

BEVERLY MASSACHUSETTS

ROCKPORT PUBLISHERS

Compiled by Gillian Blease

Contents

Pattern and Palette Sourcebook 3 is a practical guide to the application of color in pattern design to create different effects. Color can be used to demonstrate many things: mood and tension, warm and cold, density and space. We engage with and respond to color signals in our everyday lives both on a basic level (e.g., red means warning or stop) and on a much more subtle and complex level in relation to such factors as environment, activity, or food. It plays an enormous role in how we interpret meaning and function, and for the designer is a powerful tool for communication.

The origins of the patterns in this book can be found in the details of the world around us, from the mundane to the sublime. The palettes for each of the six chapters—Botanics, Mechanics, Utility, Sugar and Spice, Ancient and Modern, and Maritime—reflect color associations both inherent to the subject and as applied by society. The structure of a repeat pattern allows colors to be woven together, to create impact, to act as punctuation, or to harmonize.

Each of the patterns in the following chapters is reworked a number of times using one or more colors from the palette at the top of the page, allowing you to compare different color schemes for each pattern. When experimenting for yourself, bear in mind that, although successful combinations can come from considered decisions, many will be the result of happy accidents. Discard preconceived notions of which colors work well together and expect to be surprised!

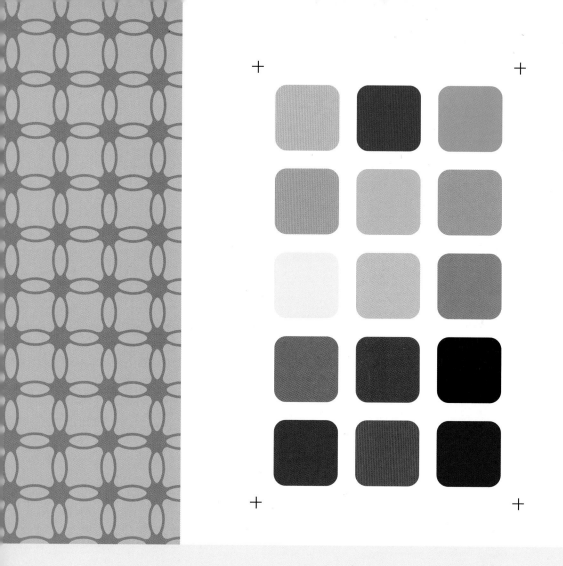

The kaleidoscopic variety of the plant kingdom is an infinite source of patterns, whether studied in detail through the microscope or at large in the landscape. The motifs and palettes reflect the luminosity, energy, and ornamentation of the living world.

Botanics

C 26	**C** 25	**C** 37	**C** 3	**C** 42	**C** 11
M 49	**M** 100	**M** 44	**M** 72	**M** 39	**M** 50
Y 82	**Y** 100	**Y** 100	**Y** 67	**Y** 59	**Y** 100
K 52	**K** 25	**K** 25	**K** 0	**K** 2	**K** 0

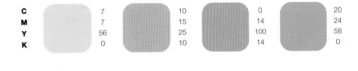

C	7		10		0		20
M	7		15		14		24
Y	56		25		100		58
K	0		10		14		0

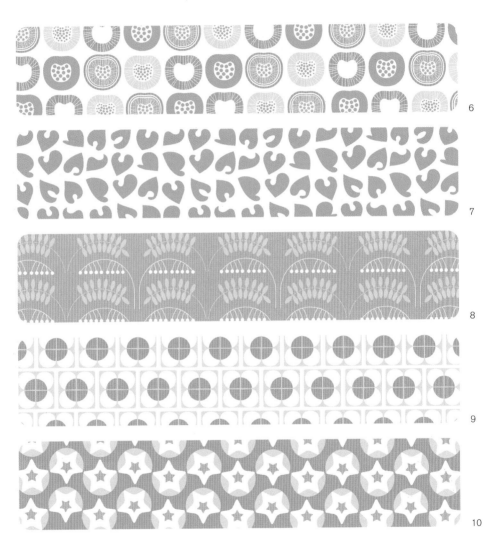

6

7

8

9

10

C	3		25		26		84		10
M	72		100		49		63		15
Y	67		100		82		94		25
K	0		25		52		40		10

11

12

13

14

15

C	0	47	25	0	7
M	14	100	100	89	7
Y	100	100	100	73	56
K	14	25	25	0	0

16

17

18

19

20

C	10	84	100	71
M	15	63	25	0
Y	25	94	50	48
K	10	40	25	0

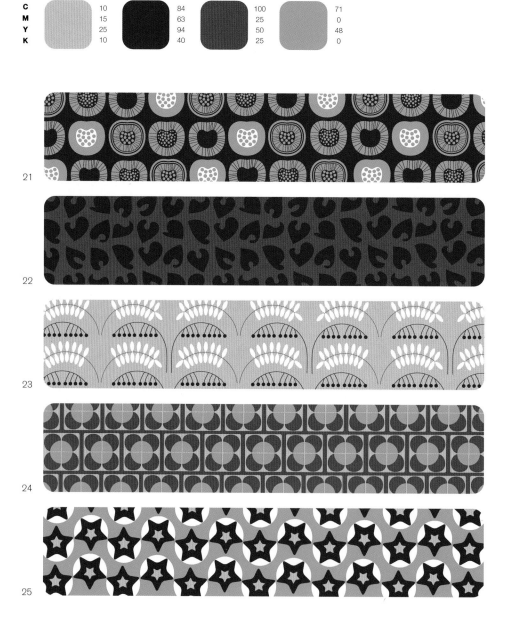

21

22

23

24

25

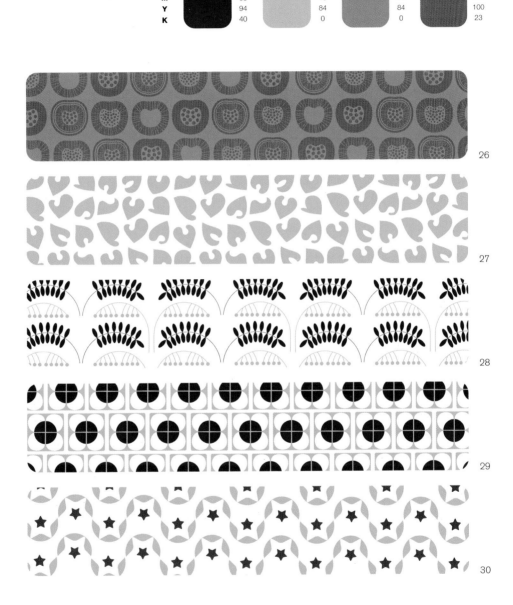

C	84		18		44		37
M	63		13		29		44
Y	94		84		84		100
K	40		0		0		23

26

27

28

29

30

C	0		10		37		11		20		42
M	89		15		44		50		75		39
Y	73		25		100		100		100		59
K	0		10		23		0		0		2

31

32

33

34

35

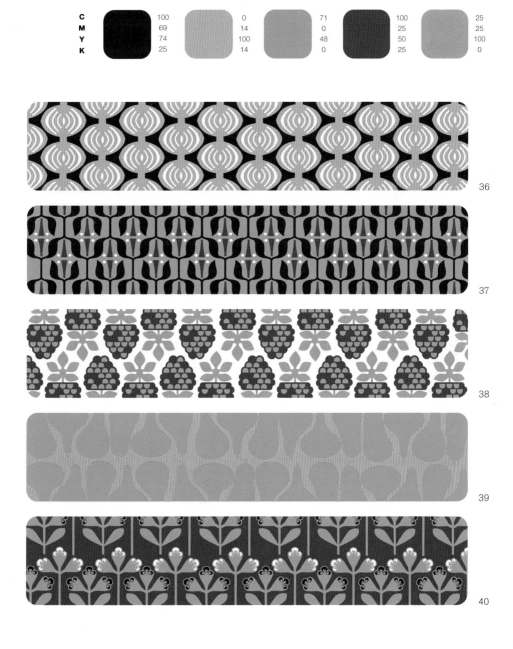

36

37

38

39

40

C		0		11		25		3		7
M		14		50		25		72		0
Y		100		100		100		67		52
K		14		0		0		0		0

41

42

43

44

45

C	26		100		10		25		37
M	49		25		15		25		44
Y	82		50		25		100		100
K	52		25		10		0		23

46

47

48

49

50

C							
C		42		26		25		26
M		39		49		100		15
Y		59		82		100		45
K		2		52		25		10

51

52

53

54

55

C	47		0		3		3
M	100		89		72		28
Y	100		73		67		52
K	25		0		0		0

56

57

58

59

60

C		26		71		18		7
M		49		0		13		0
Y		82		48		84		52
K		52		0		0		0

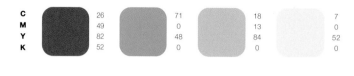

61

62

63

64

65

C	26		3		42		10
M	49		28		39		15
Y	82		52		59		25
K	52		0		2		10

66

67

68

69

70

C	84	47	26	44	100
M	63	100	15	29	25
Y	94	100	45	84	50
K	40	25	10	0	25

71

72

73

74

75

C	42		10		0		0
M	39		15		89		14
Y	59		25		73		100
K	2		10		0		14

76

77

78

79

80

C	26		84		6		100
M	15		63		0		25
Y	45		94		5		50
K	10		40		75		25

81

82

83

84

85

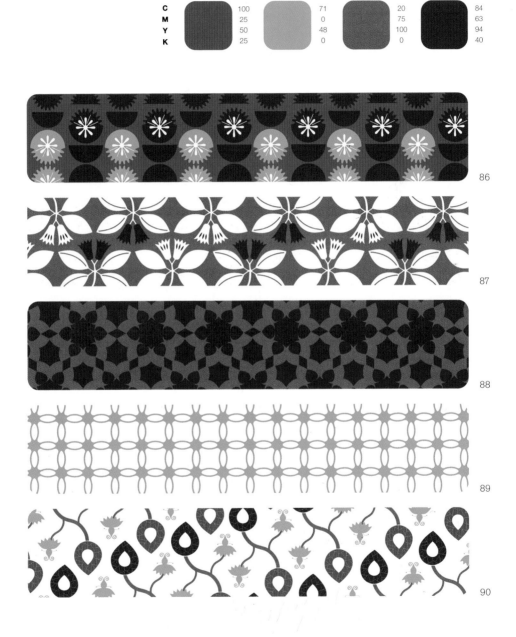

C	100		71		20		84
M	25		0		75		63
Y	50		48		100		94
K	25		0		0		40

86

87

88

89

90

C	42	25	6	20
M	39	25	0	24
Y	59	100	5	58
K	2	0	75	0

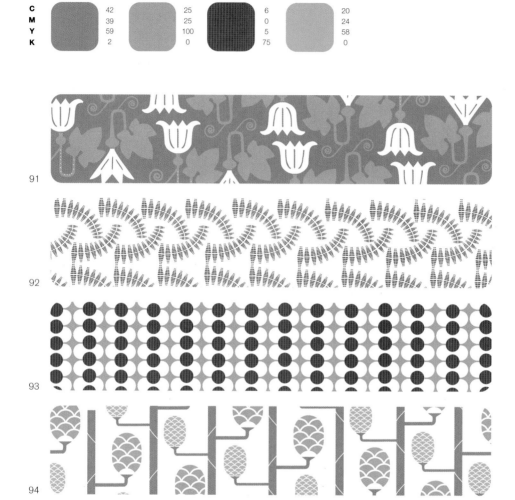

91

92

93

94

95

96

97

98

99

100

C		15		18		42		0
M		14		13		39		14
Y		100		84		59		100
K		14		0		2		14

101

102

103

104

105

C	10		37		15		6		26
M	15		44		14		0		15
Y	25		100		100		5		45
K	10		23		14		75		10

106

107

108

109

110

C	58	7	91	84
M	61	0	75	63
Y	52	52	100	94
K	0	0	56	40

111

112

113

114

115

C	10	42	20	3
M	15	39	75	28
Y	25	59	100	52
K	10	2	0	0

116

117

118

119

120

C	0		3		26		44		47
M	89		72		49		29		100
Y	73		67		82		84		100
K	0		0		52		0		25

121

122

123

124

125

C	25		100		18		25
M	100		25		13		25
Y	100		50		84		100
K	25		25		0		0

126

127

128

129

130

C	3	26	84	6	44
M	28	49	63	0	29
Y	52	82	94	5	84
K	0	52	40	75	0

131

132

133

134

135

C		47		26		7
M		100		15		0
Y		100		45		52
K		25		10		0

136

137

138

139

140

C	84	3	71
M	63	28	0
Y	94	52	48
K	40	0	0

141

142

143

144

145

C	10		42		100		26
M	15		39		25		49
Y	25		59		50		82
K	10		2		25		52

146

147

148

149

150

C	25	6	0
M	25	0	89
Y	100	5	73
K	0	75	0

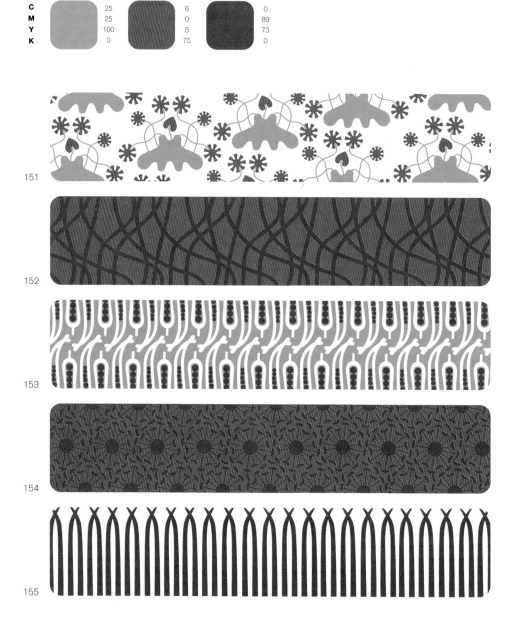

151

152

153

154

155

C	6		0		8		84		10
M	0		14		9		63		15
Y	5		100		20		94		25
K	75		14		7		40		10

156

157

158

159

160

The characteristics of machinery in motion—repetition, rhythm, and noise—translate naturally into patterns. The colors and designs in this chapter are informed by the contradictions within the subject—function and beauty, weight and delicacy, size and speed.

Mechanics

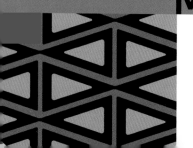

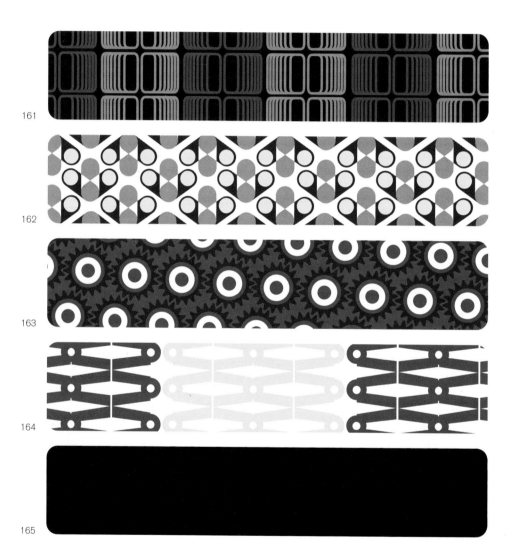

161

162

163

164

165

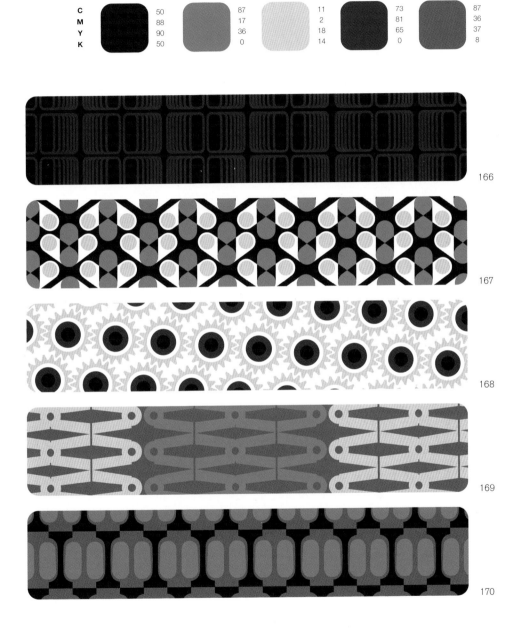

C	50		87		11		73		87
M	88		17		2		81		36
Y	90		36		18		65		37
K	50		0		14		0		8

166

167

168

169

170

C		12		12		2		11		0
M		74		62		55		2		11
Y		92		78		100		18		39
K		1		1		0		14		0

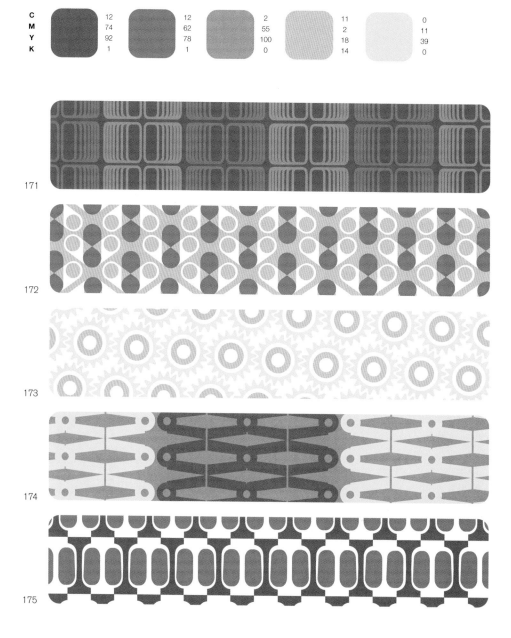

171

172

173

174

175

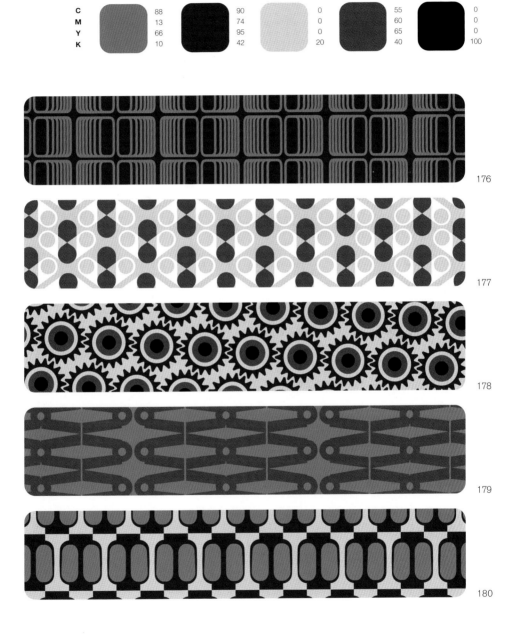

C	88		90		0		55		0
M	13		74		0		60		0
Y	66		95		0		65		0
K	10		42		20		40		100

176

177

178

179

180

C	30	40	73	0
M	84	70	81	0
Y	90	100	65	0
K	8	50	0	20

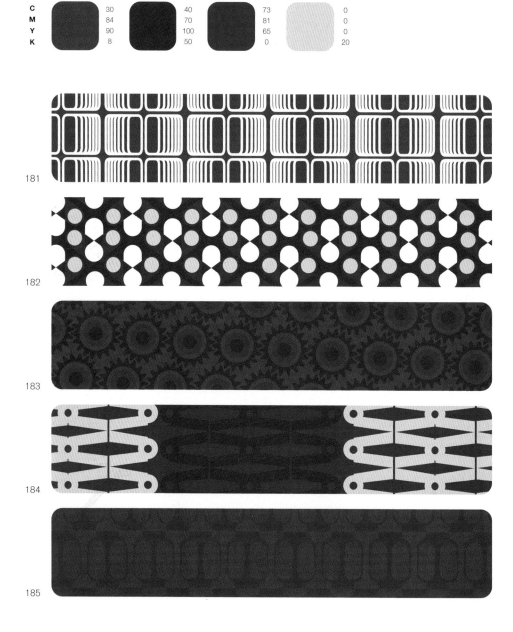

181

182

183

184

185

C	50		0		73		87
M	100		81		81		17
Y	89		89		65		36
K	50		50		0		0

186

187

188

189

190

C		11		30		50		25		50		25
M		2		14		88		40		100		25
Y		18		0		90		65		89		65
K		14		47		50		0		50		0

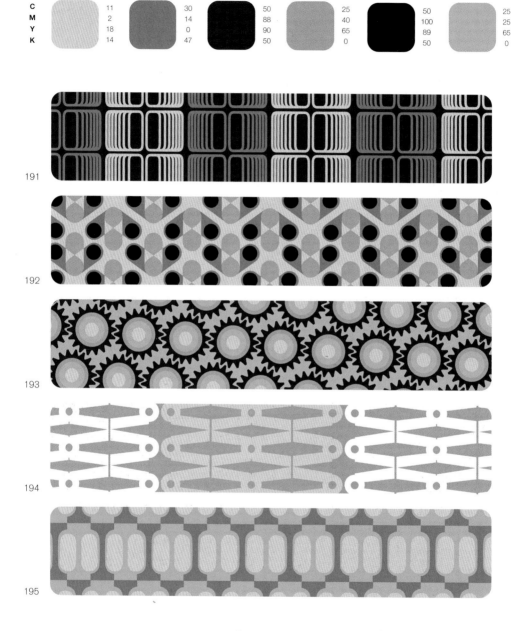

191

192

193

194

195

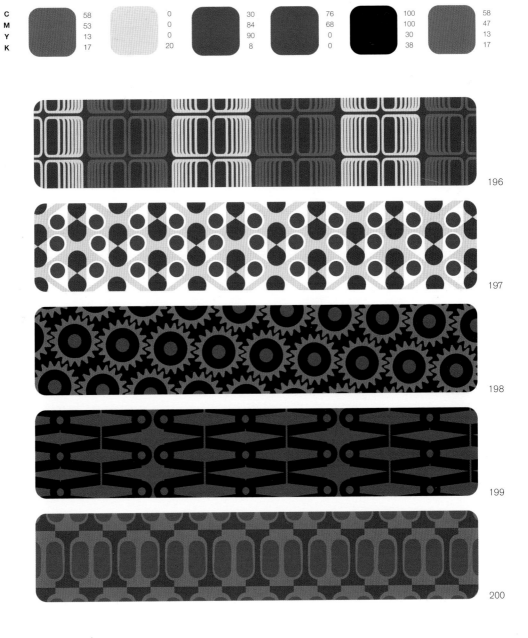

C	58		0		30		76		100		58
M	53		0		84		68		100		47
Y	13		0		90		0		30		13
K	17		20		8		0		38		17

196

197

198

199

200

C	73		90		0		0		75
M	81		74		0		11		45
Y	65		95		0		39		69
K	0		42		20		0		25

201

202

203

204

205

C	55		0		100		0		40
M	60		0		95		0		70
Y	65		0		21		0		100
K	40		40		0		100		50

206

207

208

209

210

C	73	12	90	53	17
M	81	62	74	74	21
Y	65	78	95	65	32
K	0	1	42	0	0

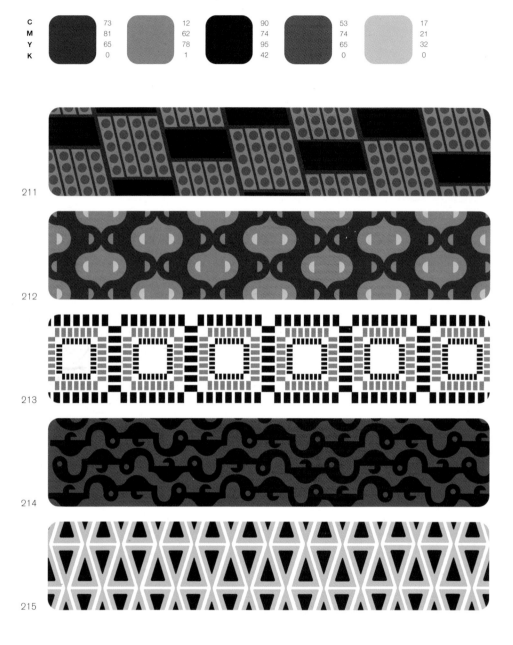

211

212

213

214

215

C		53		50		56		11		77		100
M		74		88		42		2		84		100
Y		65		90		33		18		77		30
K		0		50		47		14		19		38

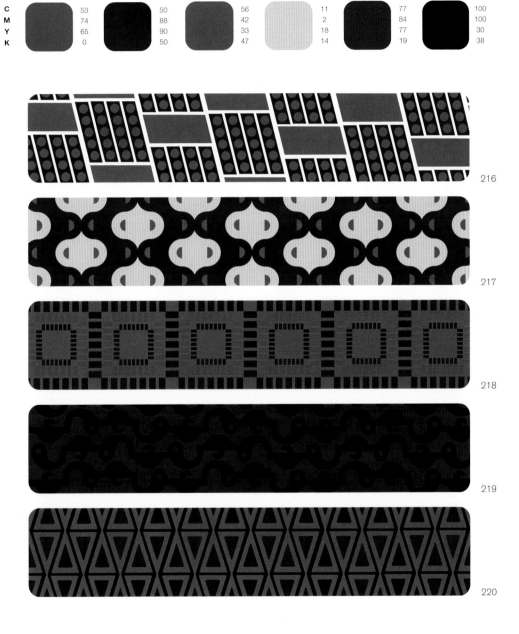

216

217

218

219

220

C 53	11	74	30	75	0
M 74	2	40	84	45	81
Y 65	18	65	89	69	89
K 0	14	0	8	25	50

221

222

223

224

225

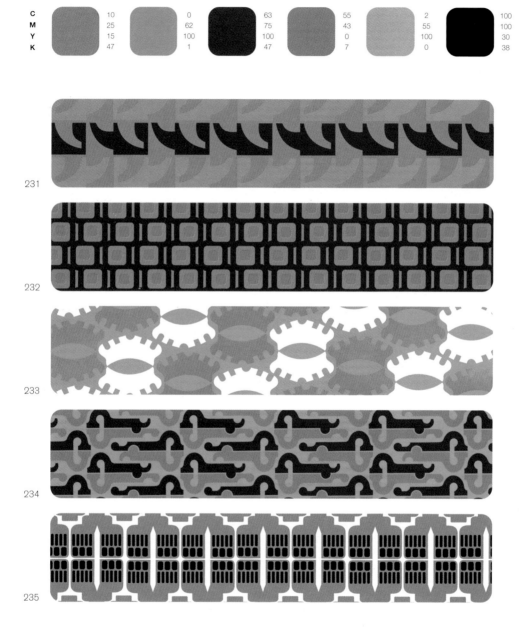

C		10		0		63		55		2		100
M		25		62		75		43		55		100
Y		15		100		100		0		100		30
K		47		1		47		7		0		38

231

232

233

234

235

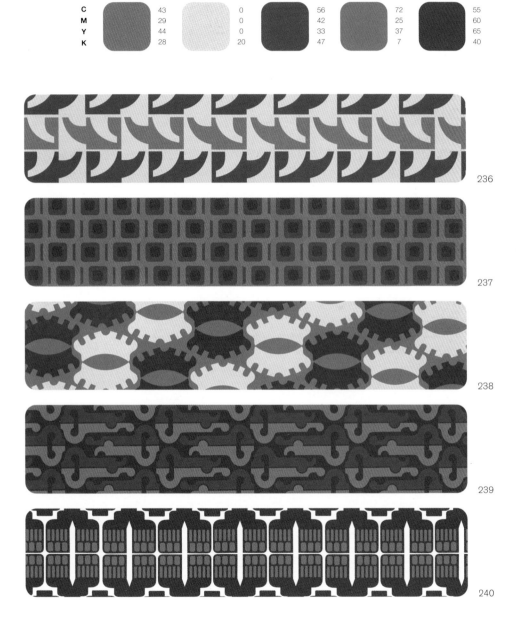

C 43 0 56 72 55
M 29 0 42 25 60
Y 44 0 33 37 65
K 28 20 47 7 40

236

237

238

239

240

C		0		10		0		19		56
M		0		25		0		15		42
Y		0		15		0		77		33
K		100		47		40		0		47

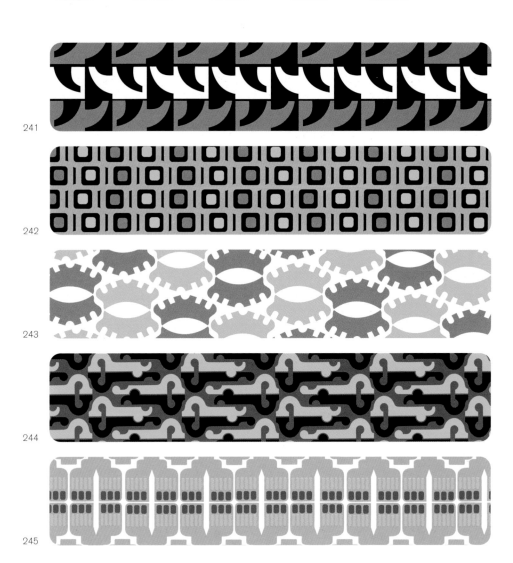

241

242

243

244

245

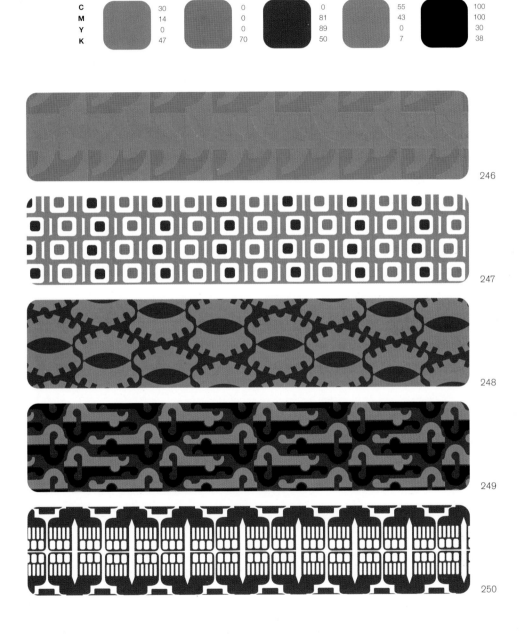

C	30		0		0		55		100
M	14		0		81		43		100
Y	0		0		89		0		30
K	47		70		50		7		38

246

247

248

249

250

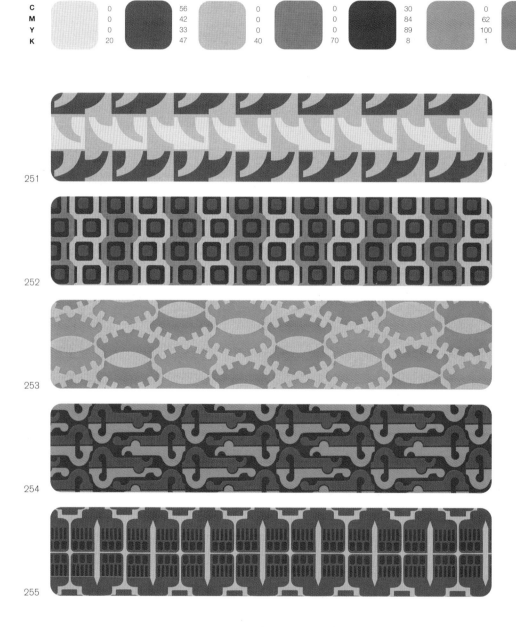

C	0		56		0		0		30		0		12
M	0		42		0		0		84		62		62
Y	0		33		0		0		89		100		78
K	20		47		40		70		8		1		1

251

252

253

254

255

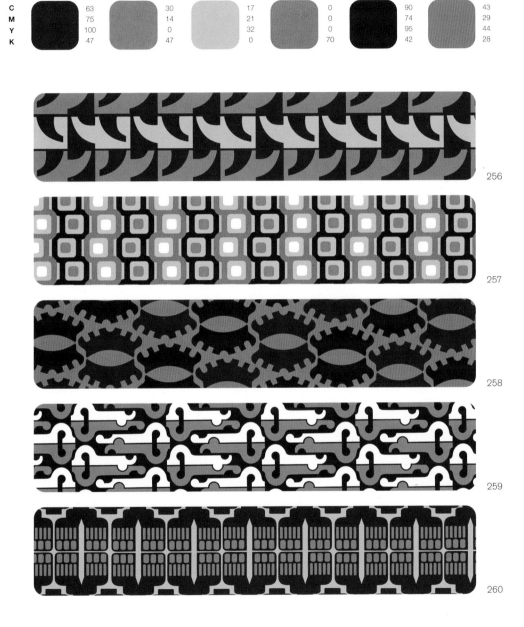

C	63	30	17	0	90	43
M	75	14	21	0	74	29
Y	100	0	32	0	95	44
K	47	47	0	70	42	28

256

257

258

259

260

C		63		55		30		0		10
M		75		43		14		11		25
Y		100		0		0		39		15
K		47		7		47		0		47

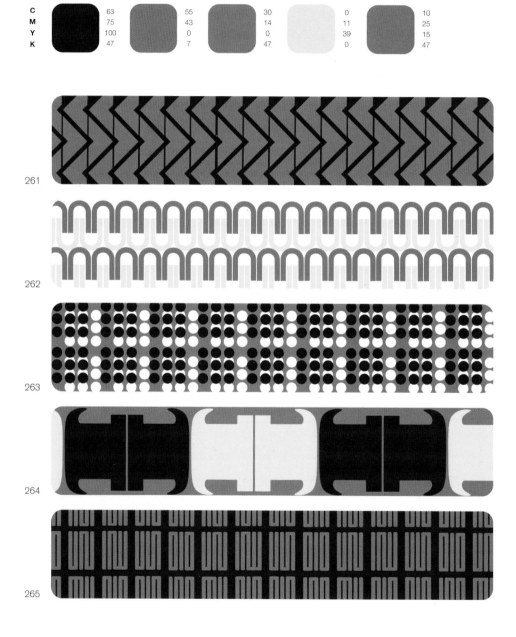

261

262

263

264

265

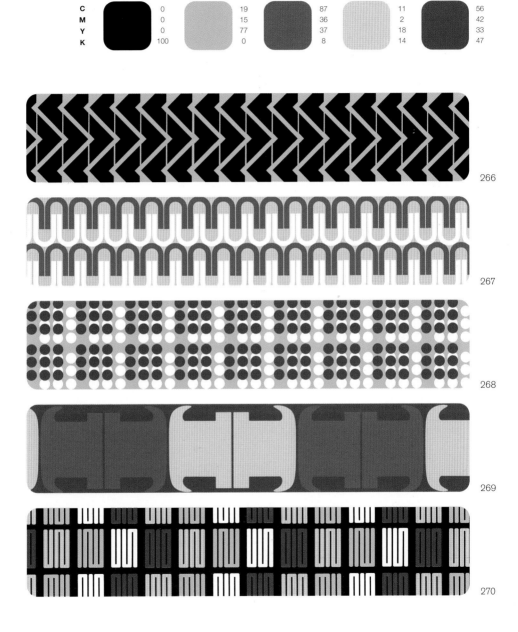

C	0		19		87		11		56
M	0		15		36		2		42
Y	0		77		37		18		33
K	100		0		8		14		47

266

267

268

269

270

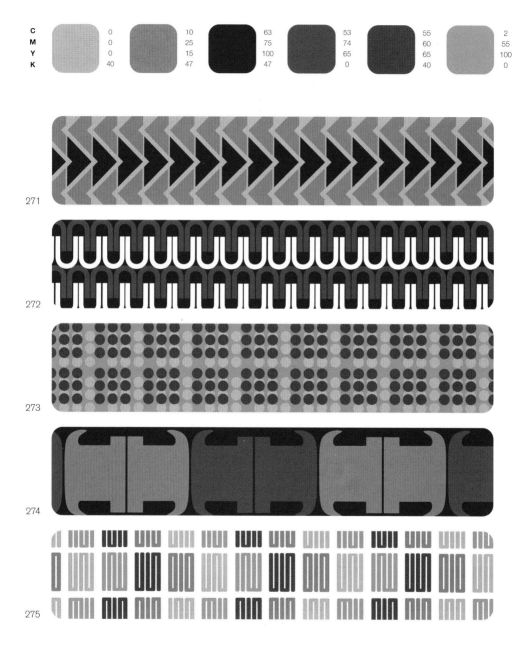

C	0	10	63	53	55	2
M	0	25	75	74	60	55
Y	0	15	100	65	65	100
K	40	47	47	0	40	0

271

272

273

274

275

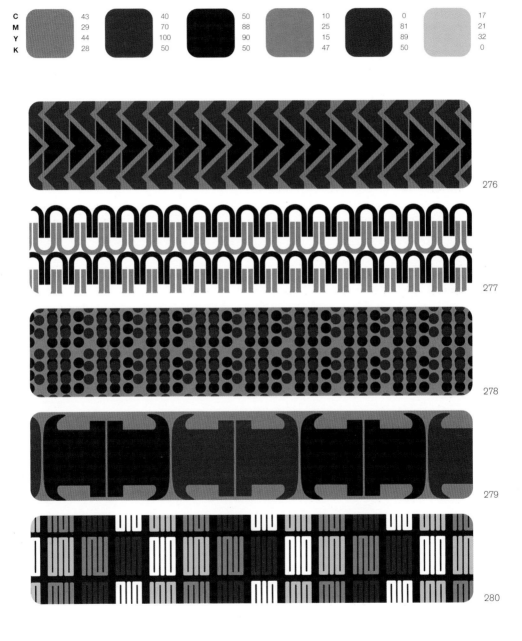

C	43		40		50		10		0		17
M	29		70		88		25		81		21
Y	44		100		90		15		89		32
K	28		50		50		47		50		0

276

277

278

279

280

C	87		50		77		25		56		0
M	17		100		84		25		42		0
Y	36		89		77		65		33		0
K	0		50		19		0		47		20

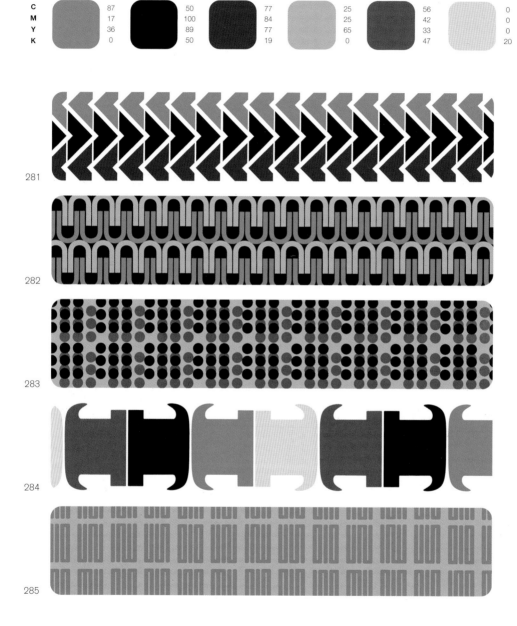

281

282

283

284

285

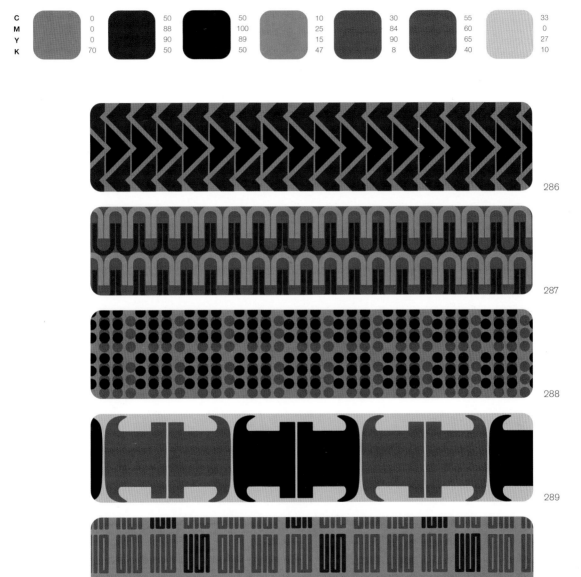

C	0	50	50	10	30	55	33
M	0	88	100	25	84	60	0
Y	0	90	89	15	90	65	27
K	70	50	50	47	8	40	10

286

287

288

289

290

C	55	25	100	100	56
M	43	40	100	95	42
Y	0	65	30	21	33
K	7	0	38	0	47

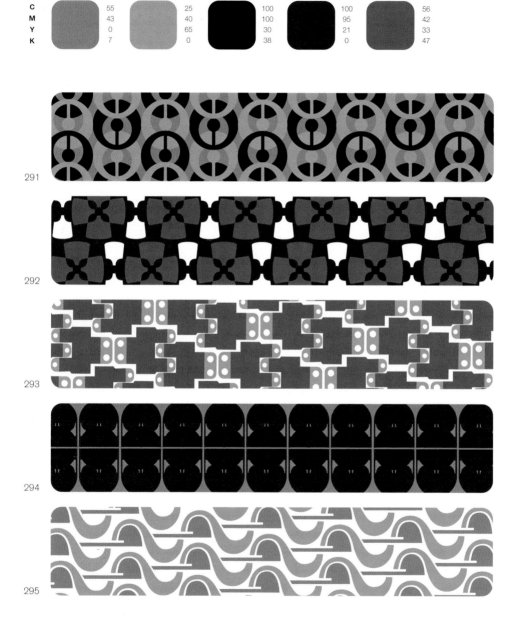

291

292

293

294

295

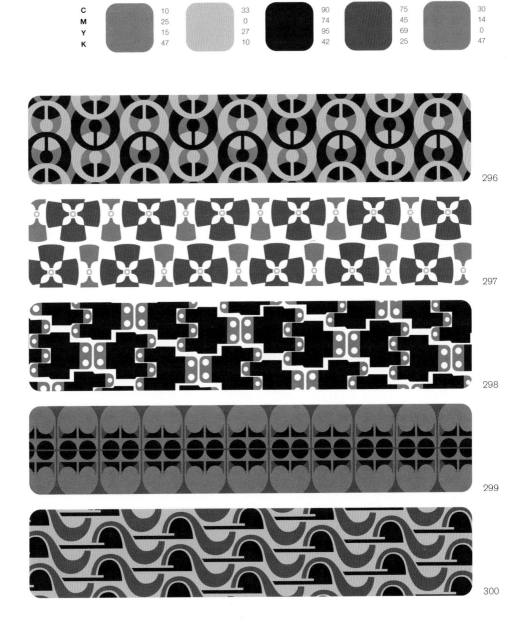

C	10		33		90		75		30
M	25		0		74		45		14
Y	15		27		95		69		0
K	47		10		42		25		47

296

297

298

299

300

C		73		90		87		33		56		75
M		81		74		36		0		42		45
Y		65		95		37		27		33		69
K		0		42		8		10		47		25

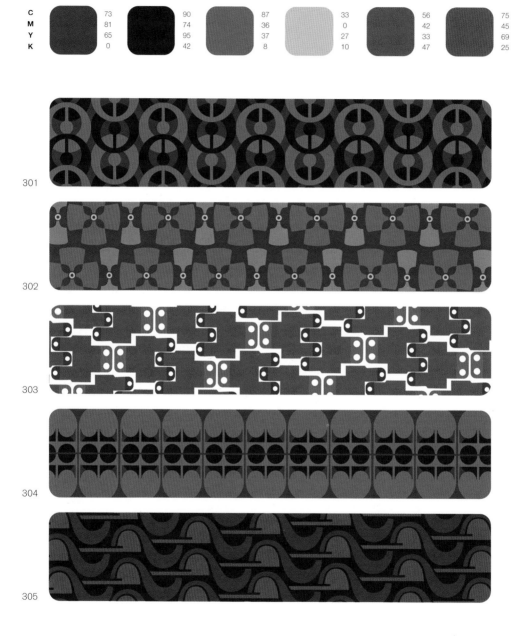

301

302

303

304

305

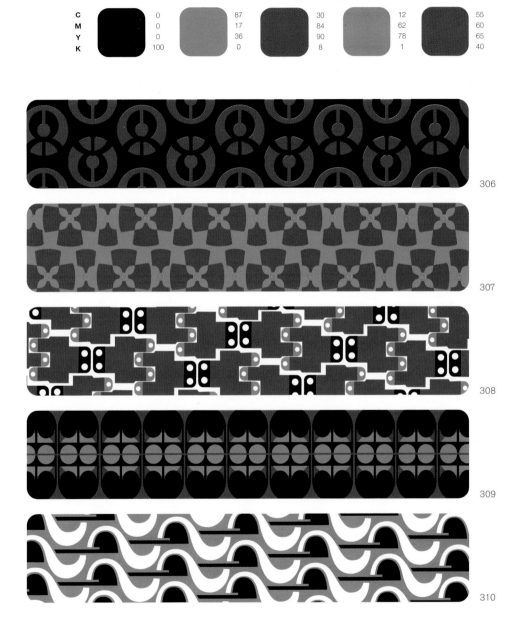

C	0		87		30		12		55
M	0		17		84		62		60
Y	0		36		90		78		65
K	100		0		8		1		40

306

307

308

309

310

C		19		11		25		63		10
M		15		2		25		75		25
Y		77		18		65		100		15
K		0		14		0		47		47

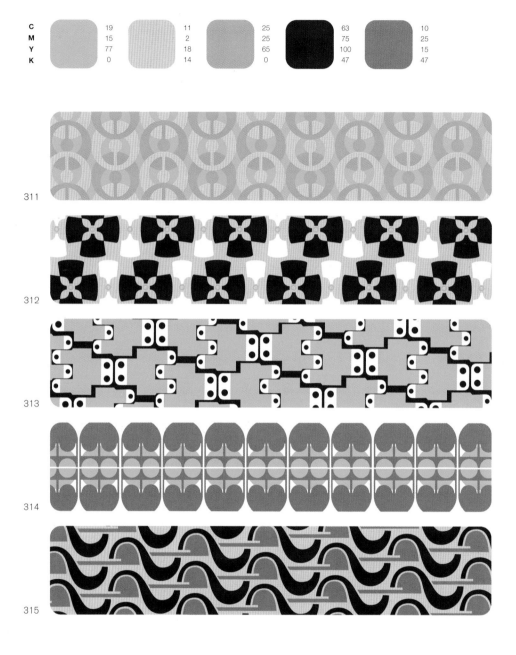

311

312

313

314

315

C	100		77		30		0
M	100		68		84		81
Y	30		0		90		89
K	38		0		8		50

316

317

318

319

320

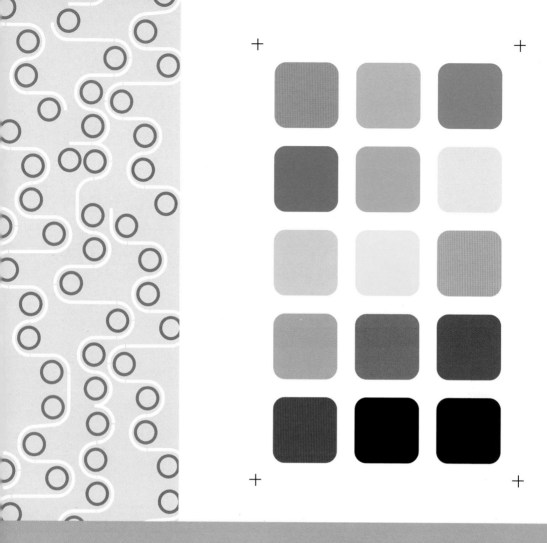

The overlooked shapes and rhythms of our daily lives are considered here. We tend to acknowledge only the purpose of a functional object, never its form. The colors in these patterns stay true to their origins, are familiar and dependable, and wipe clean.

Utility

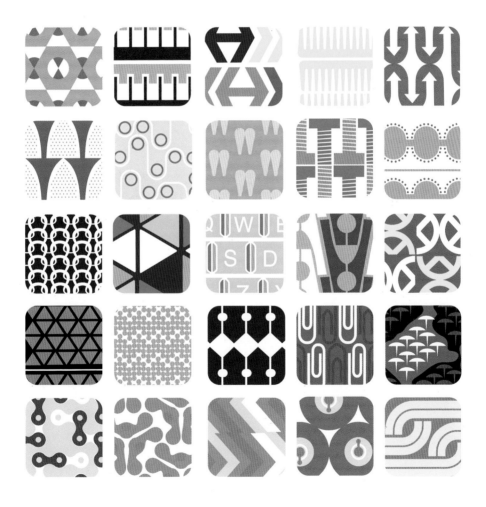

C	86		0		0		15		13		96
M	20		3		0		32		6		16
Y	26		100		0		92		25		100
K	72		0		67		27		0		0

321

322

323

324

325

C	0		0		13		61
M	50		76		6		56
Y	100		100		25		79
K	0		1		0		0

326

327

328

329

330

C 68	0	64	96	70
M 100	100	0	16	0
Y 90	100	96	100	0
K 10	0	0	0	0

331

332

333

334

335

C	0		49		36		12		86		61
M	3		20		78		14		20		56
Y	100		10		100		25		26		79
K	0		15		0		22		72		0

336

337

338

339

340

341

342

343

344

345

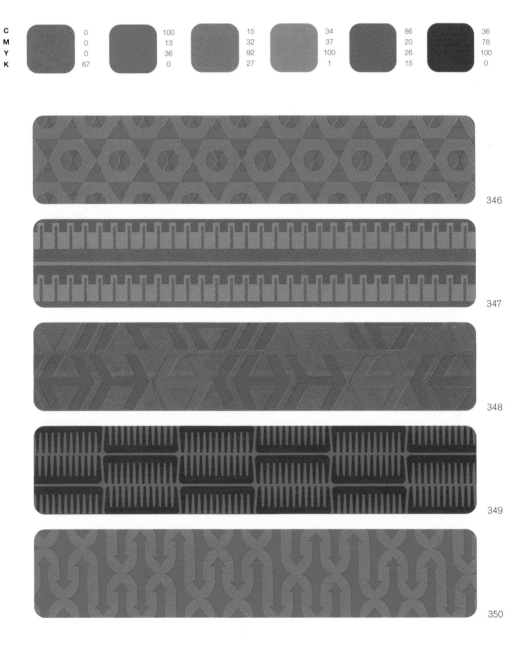

C	0		100		15		34		86		36
M	0		13		32		37		20		78
Y	0		36		92		100		26		100
K	67		0		27		1		15		0

346

347

348

349

350

C		0		12		89		61
M		100		14		37		56
Y		100		25		37		79
K		0		22		46		0

351

352

353

354

355

C	63		63		0		81		86		13
M	100		64		3		87		20		6
Y	0		0		100		66		26		25
K	60		35		0		2		58		0

356

357

358

359

360

C	89	53	81	15	0
M	37	37	87	32	0
Y	37	37	66	92	0
K	46	46	21	27	67

361

362

363

364

365

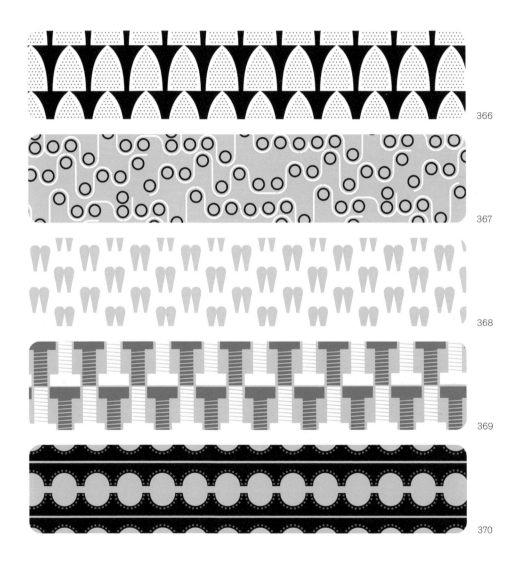

366

367

368

369

370

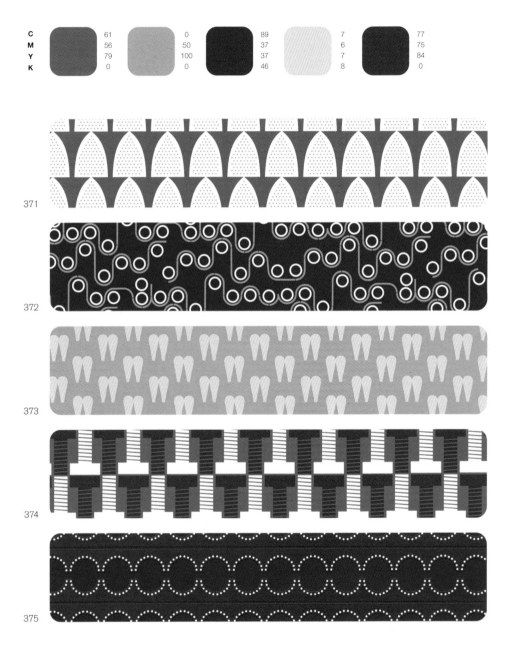

C	61	0	89	7	77
M	56	50	37	6	75
Y	79	100	37	7	84
K	0	0	46	8	0

371

372

373

374

375

C		90		13		0		12		64
M		30		6		76		14		0
Y		95		25		100		25		96
K		30		0		1		22		0

376

377

378

379

380

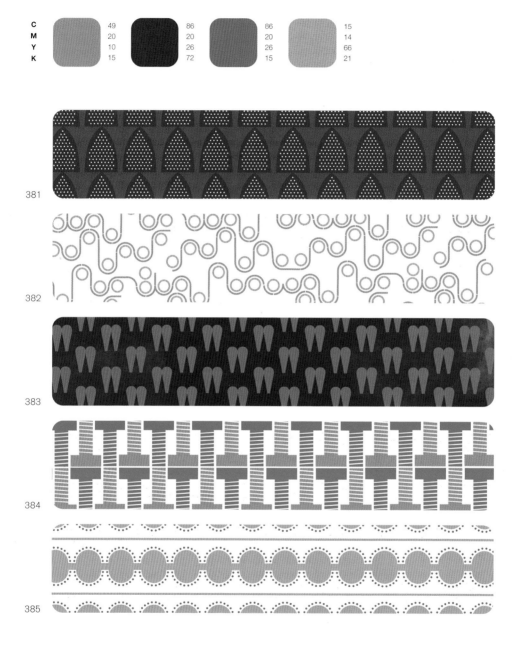

C	49	86	86	15
M	20	20	20	14
Y	10	26	26	66
K	15	72	15	21

381

382

383

384

385

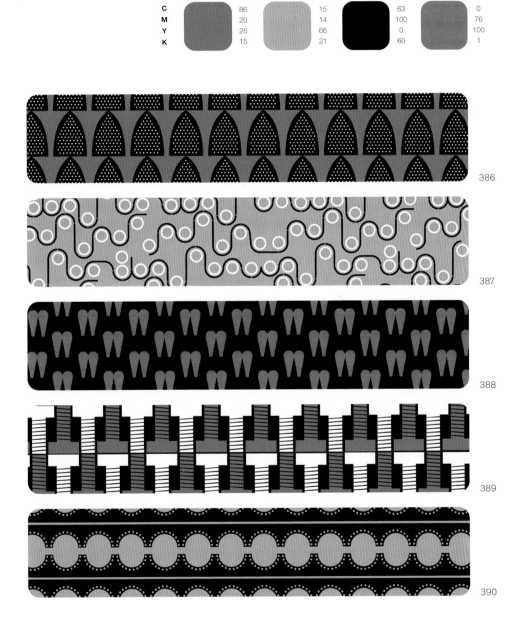

C	86		15		63		0
M	20		14		100		76
Y	26		66		0		100
K	15		21		60		1

386

387

388

389

390

C	100		36		12		15
M	13		78		14		14
Y	36		100		25		66
K	0		0		22		21

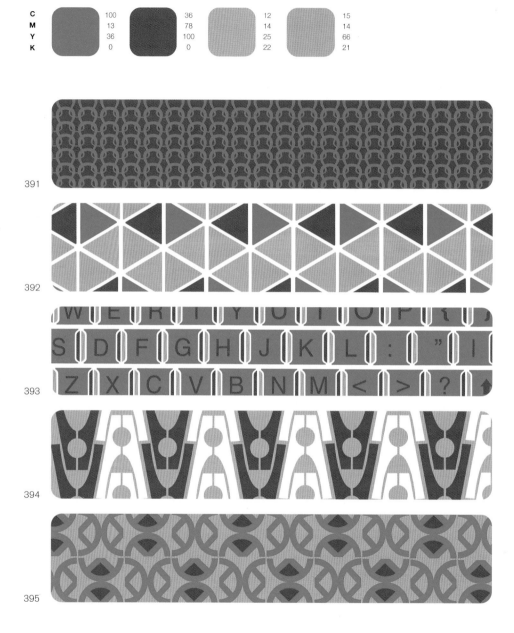

391

392

393

394

395

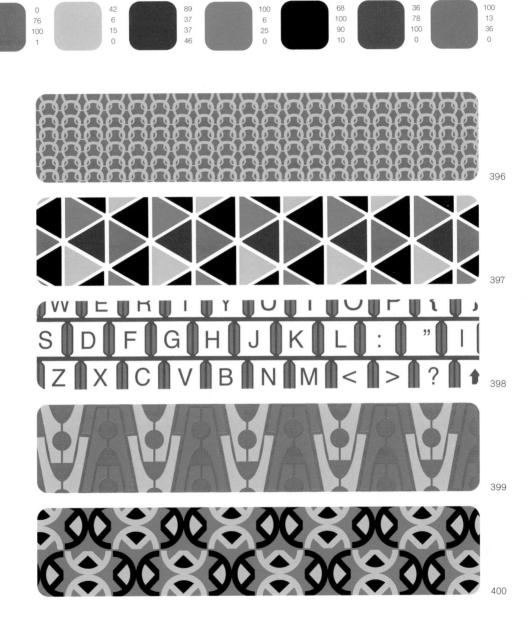

C	0	42	89	100	68	36	100
M	76	6	37	6	100	78	13
Y	100	15	37	25	90	100	36
K	1	0	46	0	10	0	0

396

397

398

399

400

C	100		15		86		10
M	13		14		20		11
Y	36		66		26		100
K	0		21		72		0

401

402

403

404

405

C	61		63		0		7
M	56		64		3		6
Y	79		0		100		7
K	0		35		0		8

406

407

408

409

410

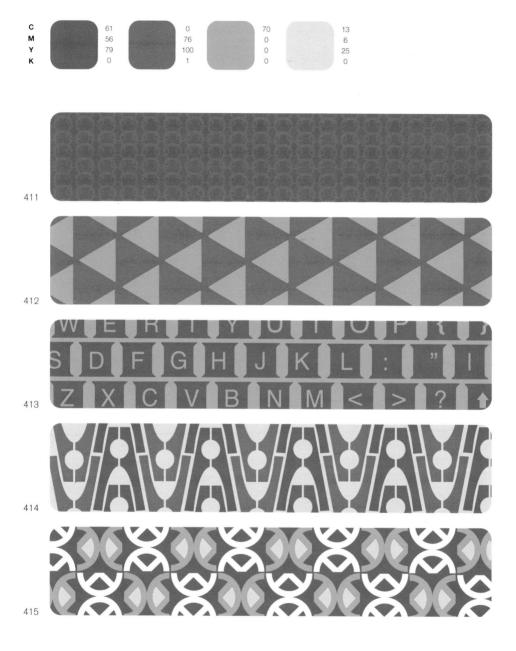

C	61	0	70	13
M	56	76	0	6
Y	79	100	0	25
K	0	1	0	0

411

412

413

414

415

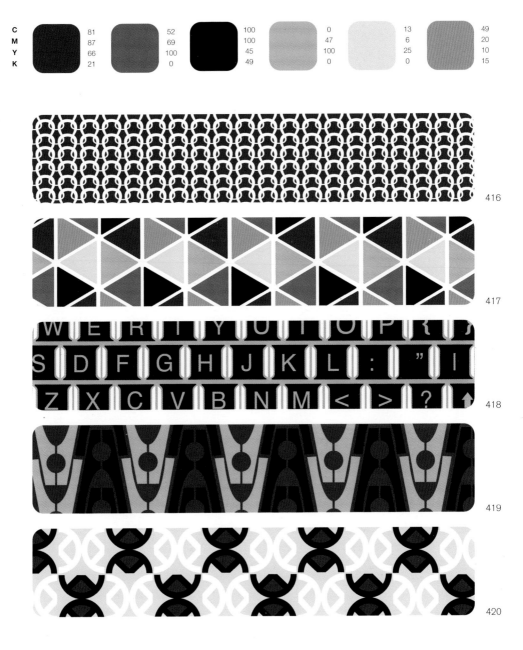

C	M	Y	K
81	87	66	21
52	69	100	0
100	100	45	49
0	47	100	0
13	6	25	0
49	20	10	15

416

417

418

419

420

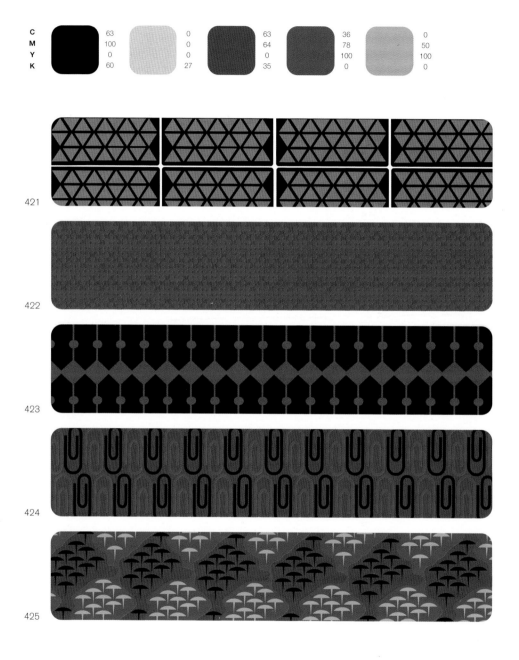

C	63	0	63	36	0
M	100	0	64	78	50
Y	0	0	0	100	100
K	60	27	35	0	0

421

422

423

424

425

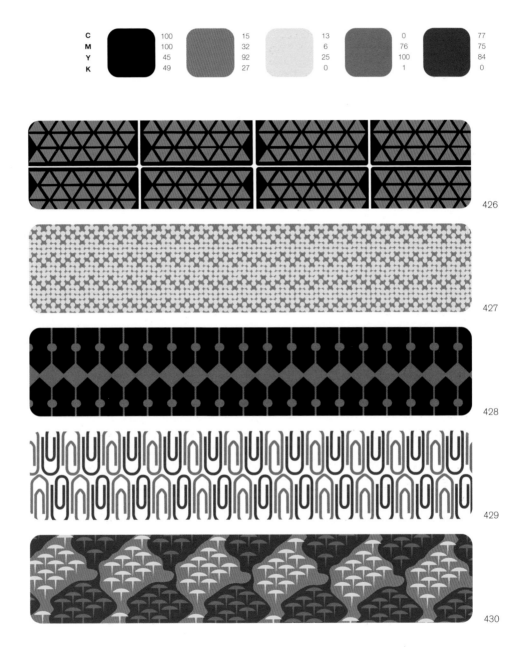

426

427

428

429

430

C	15		68		89		61
M	14		100		37		56
Y	66		90		37		79
K	21		10		27		0

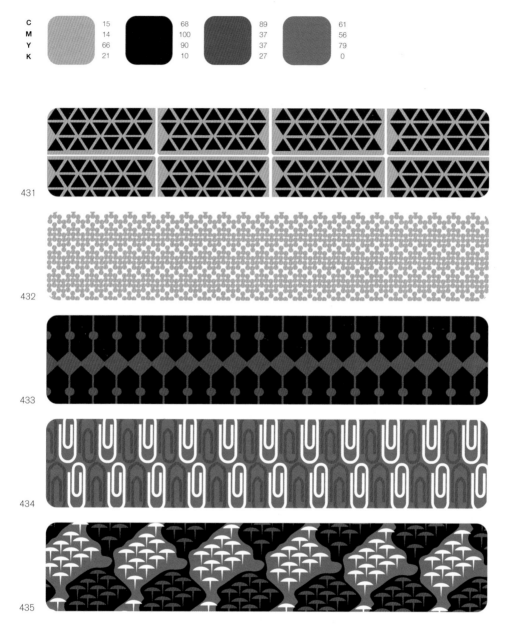

431

432

433

434

435

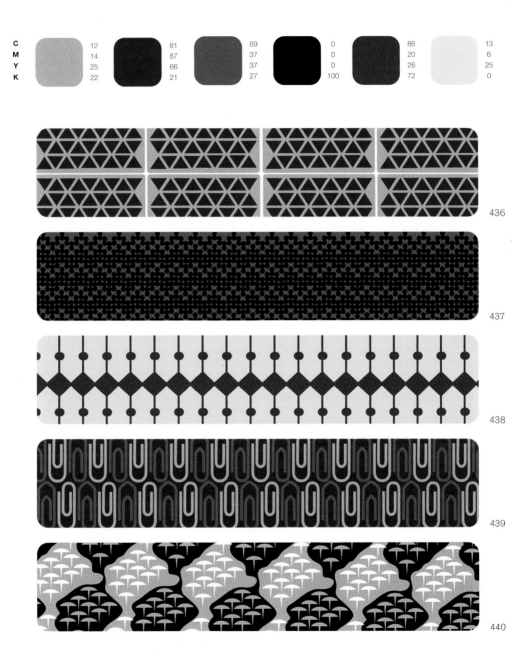

C 12 81 89 0 86 13
M 14 87 37 0 20 6
Y 25 66 37 0 26 25
K 22 21 27 100 72 0

436

437

438

439

440

C		96		36		53		68
M		16		78		37		100
Y		100		100		37		90
K		0		0		46		10

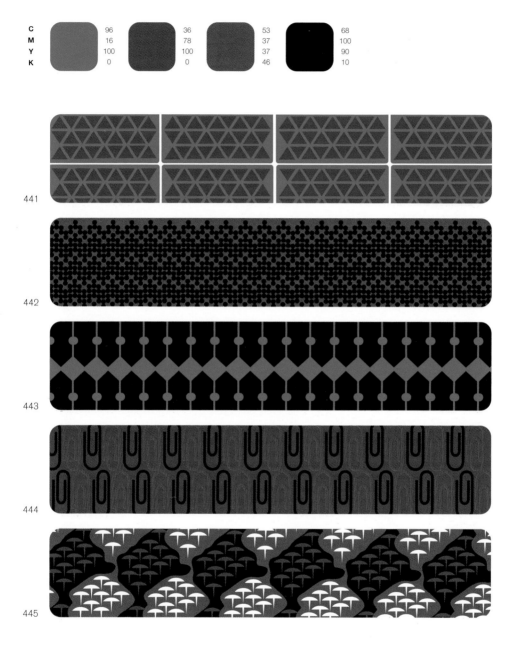

441

442

443

444

445

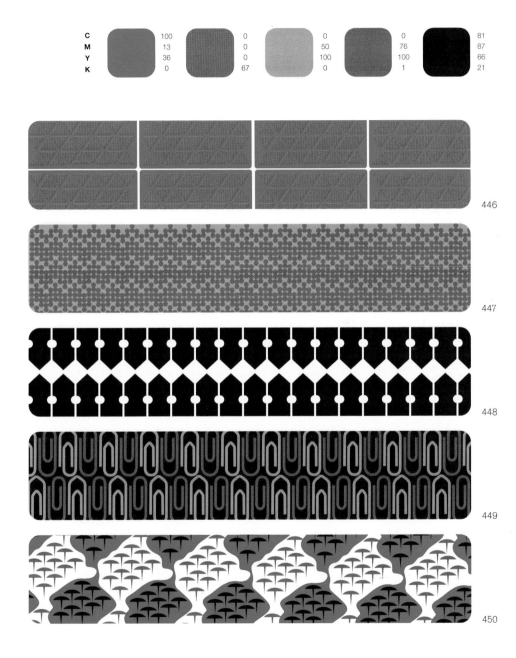

C 100 0 0 0 81
M 13 0 50 76 87
Y 36 0 100 100 66
K 0 67 0 0 21

446

447

448

449

450

C	64		0		42		61
M	0		100		6		56
Y	96		100		15		79
K	0		0		0		0

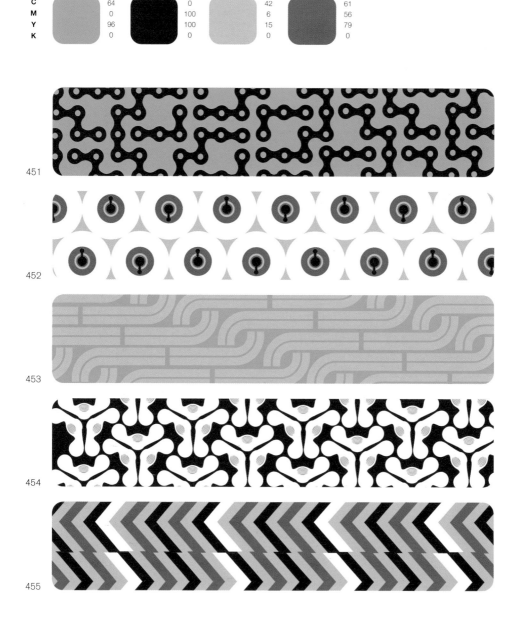

451

452

453

454

455

C		15
M		14
Y		66
K		21

81
87
66
21

25
11
11
11

13
6
25
0

90
30
95
30

68
100
90
10

456

457

458

459

460

C	13		63		0		15
M	6		64		76		32
Y	25		0		100		92
K	0		35		1		27

461

462

463

464

465

C	10		6		0		0
M	11		0		0		3
Y	100		56		0		100
K	0		0		100		0

466

467

468

469

470

C	63	36	12	0	13
M	100	78	14	100	6
Y	0	100	25	100	25
K	60	0	22	0	0

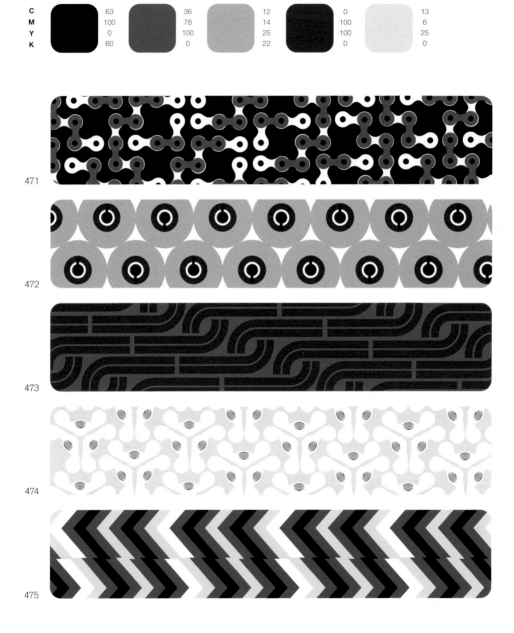

471

472

473

474

475

C	49	15	81	6	13
M	20	32	87	0	6
Y	10	92	66	56	25
K	15	27	21	0	0

476

477

478

479

480

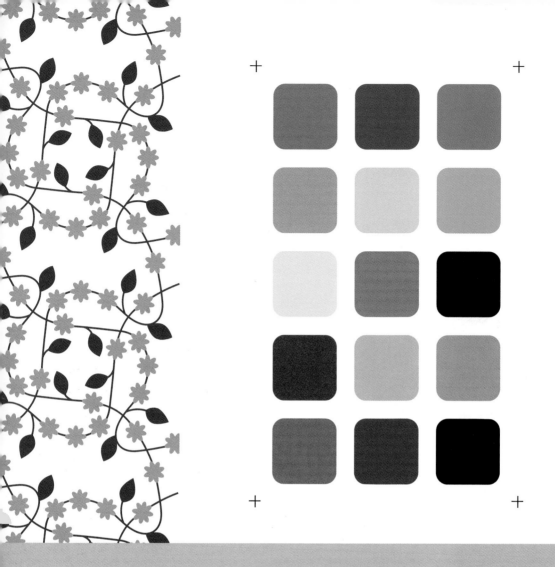

These patterns focus on luxury, indulgence, and the senses —taste, scent, and texture—reflected in the curving outlines and rich warm palette. In this context the discipline of a repeat pattern allows the designer to be truly frivolous without losing sight of structure.

Sugar and Spice

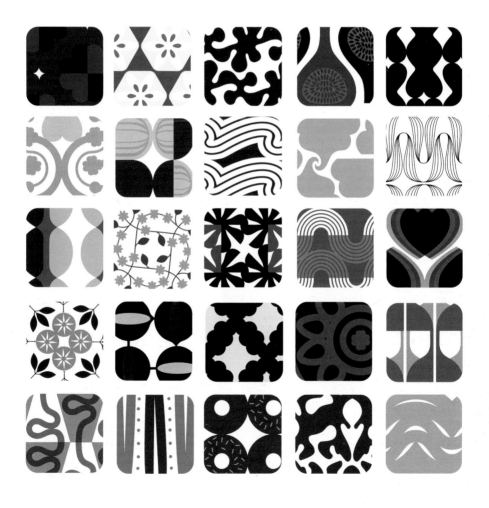

C	21	82	77	2	0
M	96	77	100	16	81
Y	16	90	64	17	50
K	0	0	24	0	0

481

482

483

484

485

C 52	12	0	31	79
M 72	13	94	100	100
Y 100	22	40	100	82
K 0	0	0	0	0

486

487

488

489

490

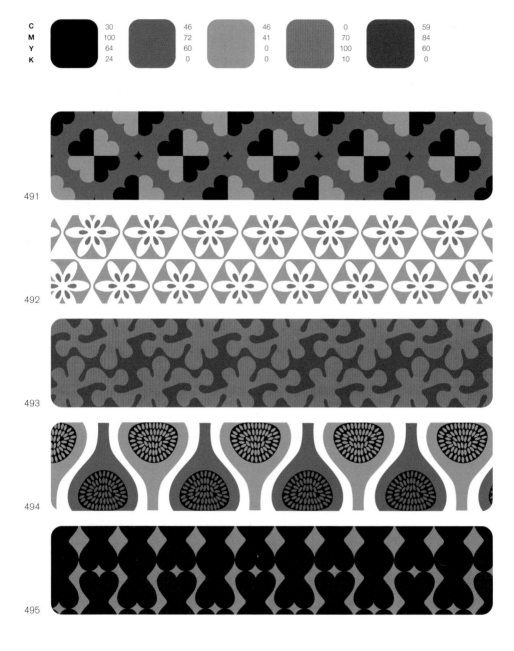

C	30	46	46	0	59
M	100	72	41	70	84
Y	64	60	0	100	60
K	24	0	0	10	0

491

492

493

494

495

C		16		52		20		0		13
M		78		72		91		0		33
Y		0		100		0		65		100
K		0		0		0		0		0

496

497

498

499

500

C 78	78	0	7	30
M 60	85	16	72	100
Y 61	94	19	51	64
K 0	0	0	0	24

501

502

503

504

505

C	13		59		29		16		30
M	81		84		100		78		100
Y	76		60		100		0		64
K	0		0		0		0		24

506

507

508

509

510

C	50		12		77		13
M	96		13		100		33
Y	20		22		64		100
K	0		0		24		0

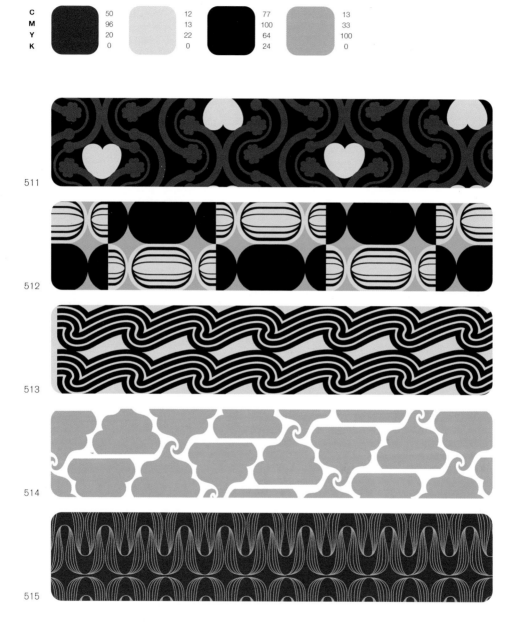

511

512

513

514

515

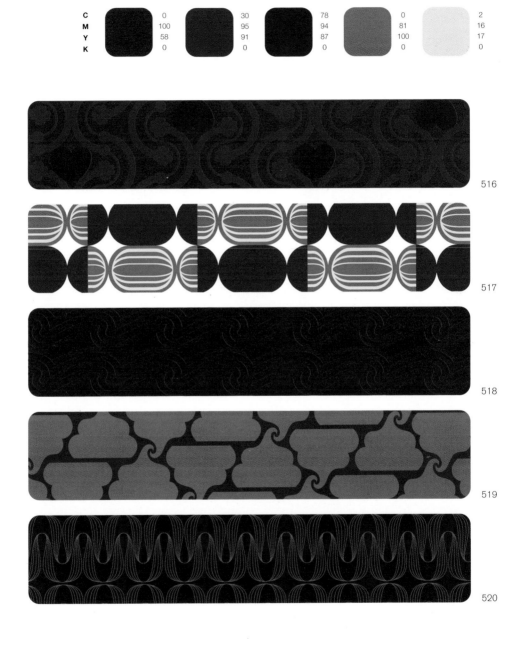

C	0		30		78		0		2
M	100		95		94		81		16
Y	58		91		87		100		17
K	0		0		0		0		0

516

517

518

519

520

C	34		0		21		79
M	33		38		96		100
Y	71		46		16		82
K	0		0		10		0

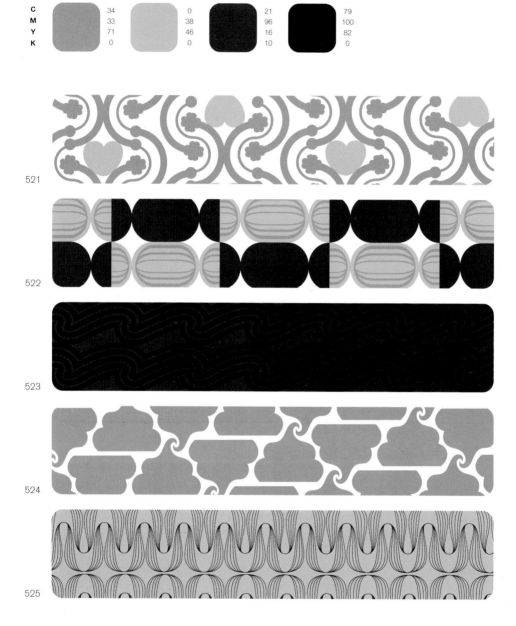

521

522

523

524

525

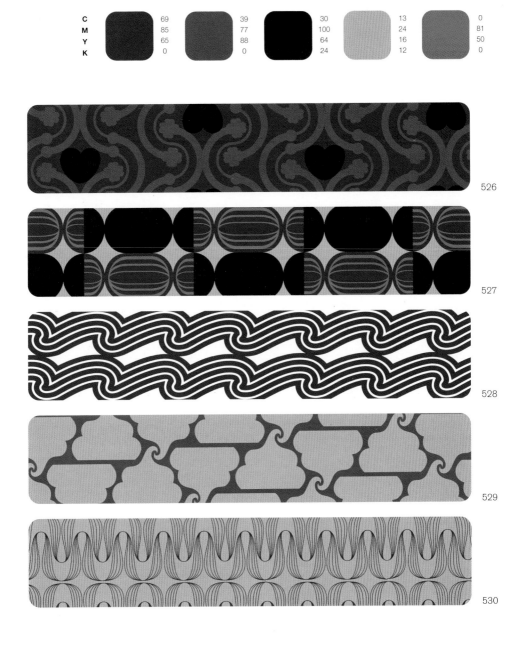

C	69		39		30		13		0
M	85		77		100		24		81
Y	65		88		64		16		50
K	0		0		24		12		0

526

527

528

529

530

C		77		52		0		32
M		100		72		100		42
Y		64		100		10		59
K		24		0		0		0

531

532

533

534

535

C	60		16		79		0
M	59		99		93		81
Y	75		100		82		50
K	0		0		0		0

536

537

538

539

540

C	59	22	21	77	78
M	84	51	96	100	60
Y	60	0	16	64	61
K	0	0	10	24	0

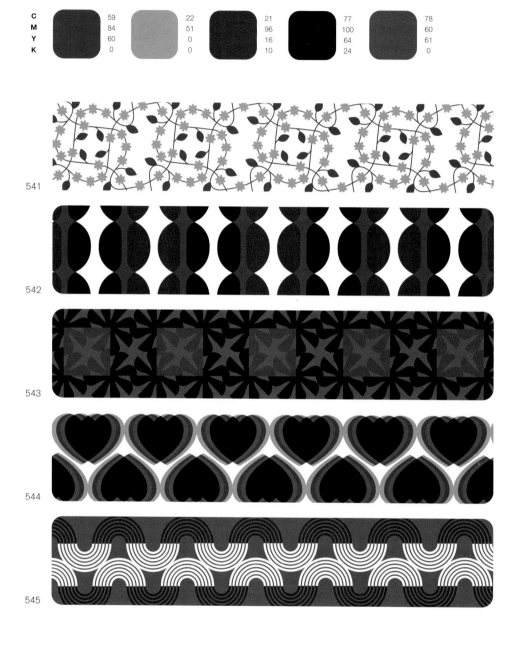

541

542

543

544

545

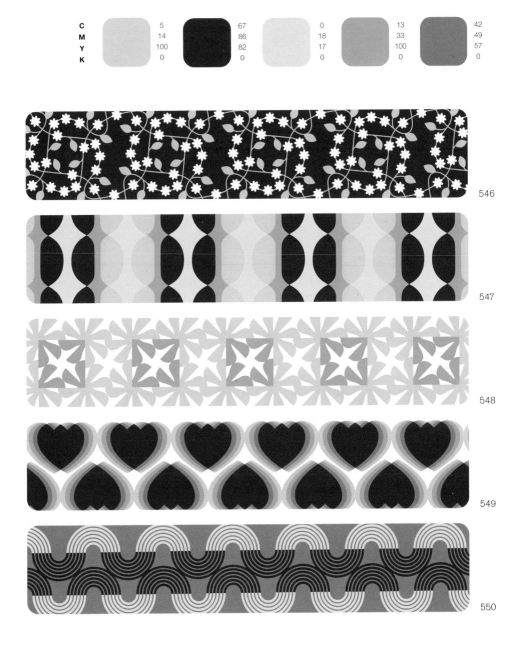

C	5	67	0	13	42
M	14	86	18	33	49
Y	100	82	17	100	57
K	0	0	0	0	0

546

547

548

549

550

C	78		77		31		50		0
M	67		100		100		61		81
Y	61		64		52		61		50
K	0		24		0		0		0

551

552

553

554

555

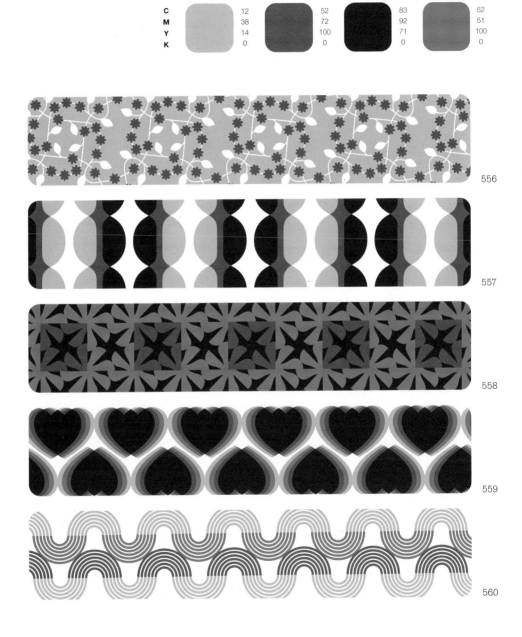

C	12		52		83		52
M	38		72		92		51
Y	14		100		71		100
K	0		0		0		0

556

557

558

559

560

C		78		16		0		50
M		85		78		76		96
Y		94		0		100		20
K		0		0		10		0

561

562

563

564

565

C 25	0	52	0	40
M 9	81	72	16	48
Y 75	22	100	19	100
K 0	0	0	0	50

566

567

568

569

570

C	77		25		67		2		0
M	100		39		79		72		16
Y	64		40		0		83		19
K	24		0		0		0		0

571

572

573

574

575

C	13	45	0	63	25
M	33	67	0	85	39
Y	100	15	65	41	40
K	0	0	0	0	0

576

577

578

579

580

C		31		39		67		20
M		100		42		86		91
Y		52		92		82		0
K		0		0		0		0

581

582

583

584

585

C	50		22		78		78
M	96		51		60		20
Y	20		0		61		61
K	0		0		0		0

586

587

588

589

590

C	21	56	20	12	31
M	33	100	91	38	100
Y	100	59	0	14	52
K	0	25	0	0	0

591

592

593

594

595

C	25	0	77	5
M	39	100	100	44
Y	40	100	64	0
K	0	0	24	0

596

597

598

599

600

C	0		0		62		39
M	81		100		50		95
Y	50		46		0		97
K	0		0		0		0

601

602

603

604

605

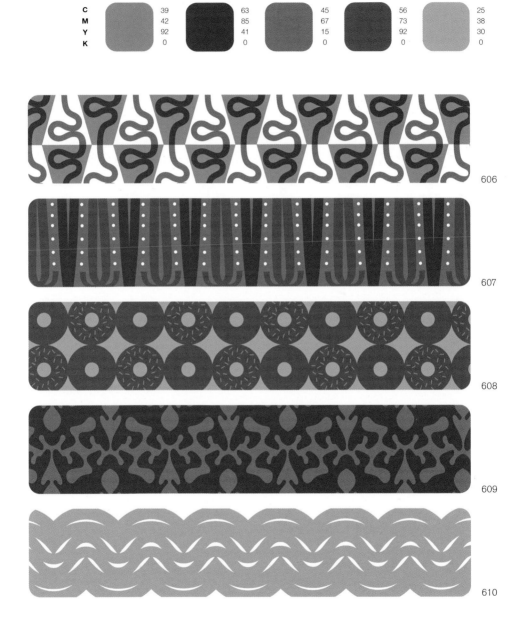

C	39	
M	42	
Y	92	
K	0	

63
85
41
0

45
67
15
0

56
73
92
0

25
38
30
0

606

607

608

609

610

C		22		17		2		50
M		51		82		27		96
Y		0		89		61		20
K		0		0		0		0

611

612

613

614

615

C	74	69	62	62	39	46
M	90	70	50	69	95	41
Y	91	0	0	15	97	0
K	8	0	0	0	0	0

616

617

618

619

620

C	78	0	12	78	30
M	60	100	13	85	100
Y	61	58	22	94	64
K	0	0	0	0	24

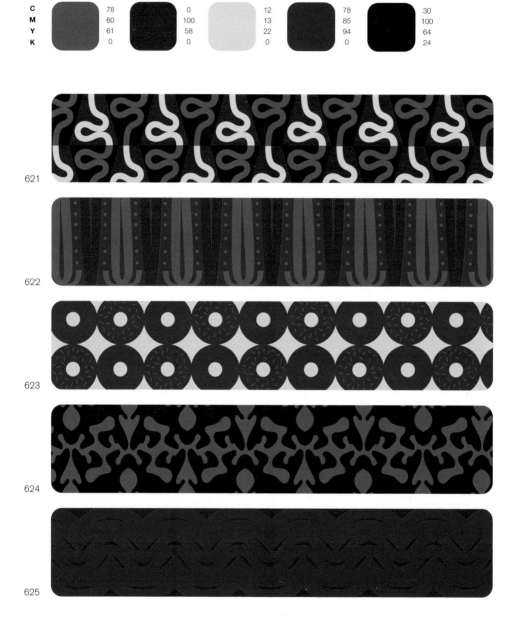

621

622

623

624

625

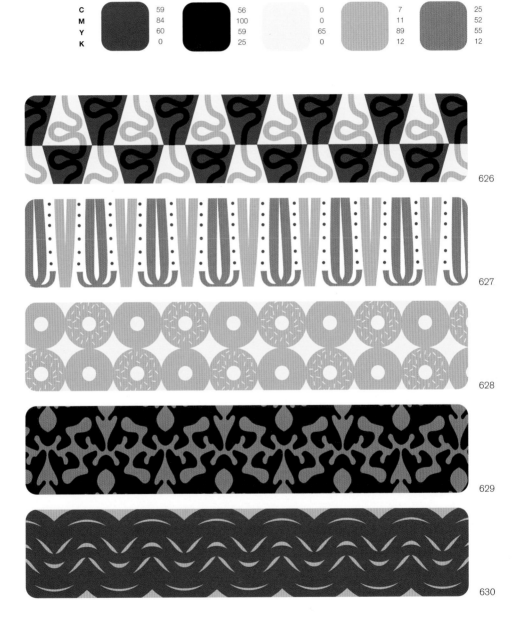

C	59		56		0		7		25
M	84		100		0		11		52
Y	60		59		65		89		55
K	0		25		0		12		12

626

627

628

629

630

		67		0		22		0
C		67		0		22		0
M		86		100		84		16
Y		82		0		85		19
K		0		0		0		0

631

632

633

634

635

C	50		79		0		11		0
M	86		100		72		69		85
Y	88		82		63		10		10
K	0		0		0		47		47

636

637

638

639

640

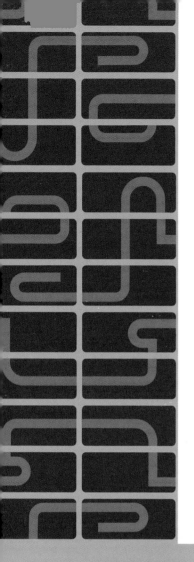

How do we register old and new? Do certain contours belong to certain eras, or do we recognize age by texture, color, and patina? Perhaps the pattern is naïve or slick, geometric or aerodynamic, warm in tone or cold. These designs consider the visual attributes of past and future and how time shapes the world around us.

Ancient and Modern

C		25		11		5		19		47
M		26		0		26		55		69
Y		90		90		90		100		100
K		0		0		0		0		0

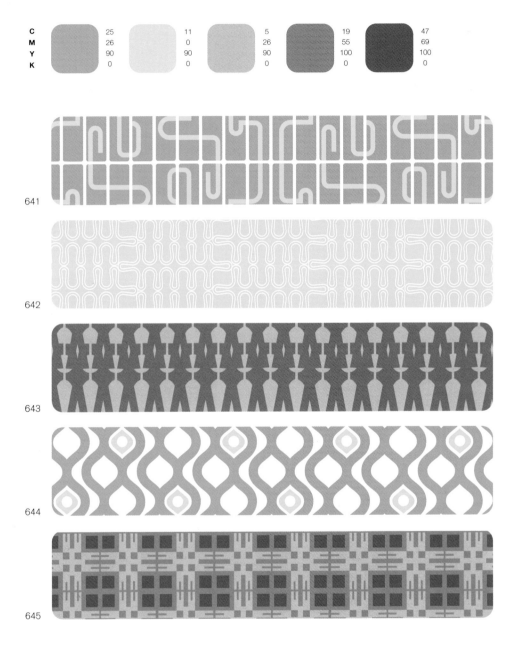

641

642

643

644

645

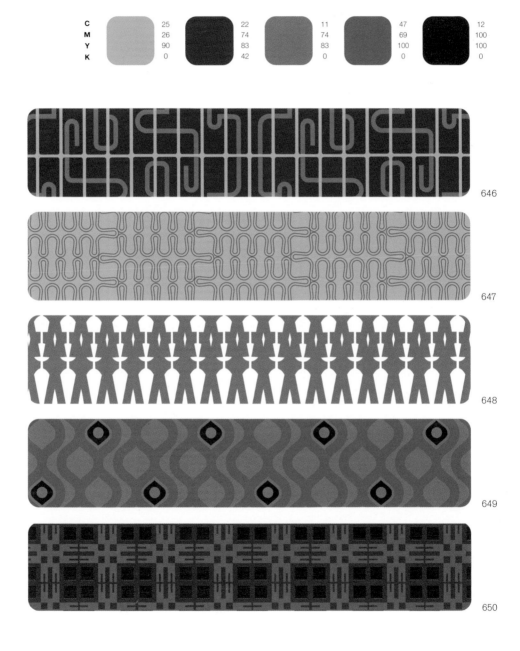

C	25		22		11		47		12
M	26		74		74		69		100
Y	90		83		83		100		100
K	0		42		0		0		0

646

647

648

649

650

C		69		71		40		25
M		53		94		56		40
Y		41		81		77		89
K		3		3		3		3

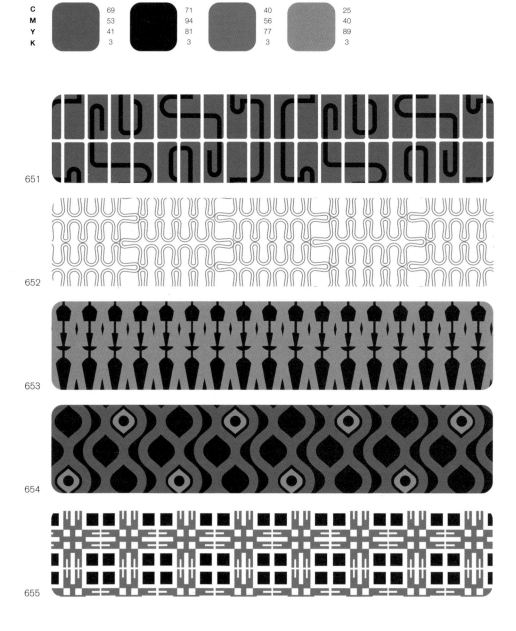

651

652

653

654

655

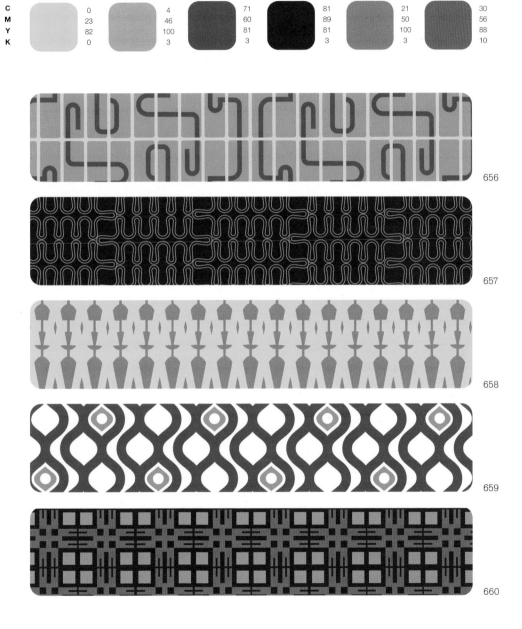

C		0		4		71		81		21		30
M		23		46		60		89		50		56
Y		82		100		81		81		100		88
K		0		3		3		3		3		10

656

657

658

659

660

C		0		30		25		59		30
M		29		41		78		71		56
Y		40		77		100		100		88
K		0		3		0		0		10

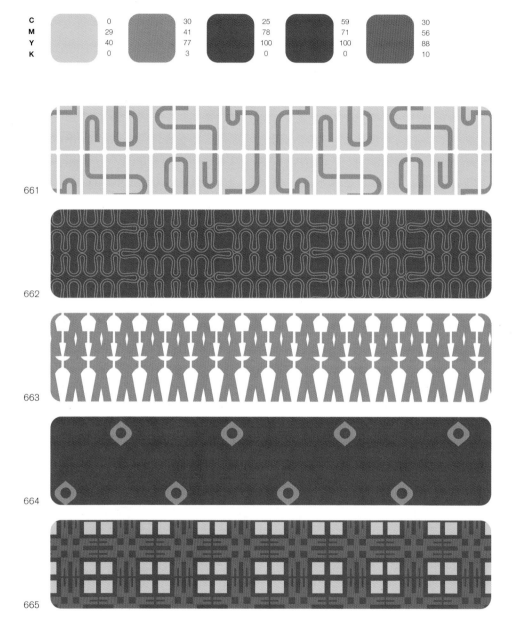

661

662

663

664

665

C		30		9		71		46		17
M		41		14		88		56		42
Y		77		100		81		94		100
K		3		0		3		0		3

666

667

668

669

670

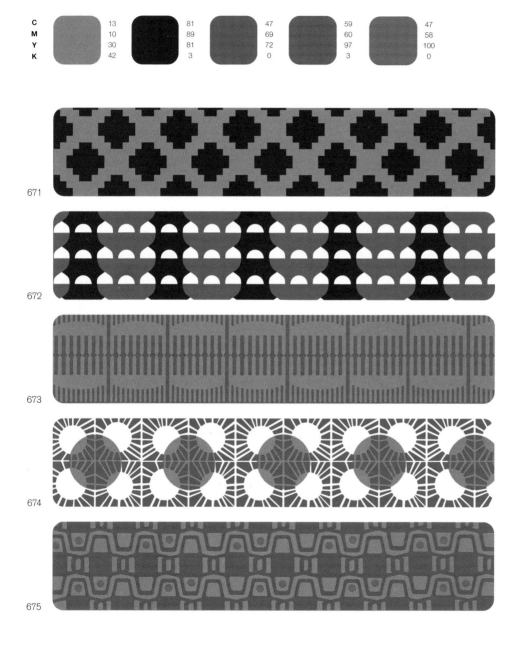

C	13		81		47		59		47
M	10		89		69		60		58
Y	30		81		72		97		100
K	42		3		0		3		0

671

672

673

674

675

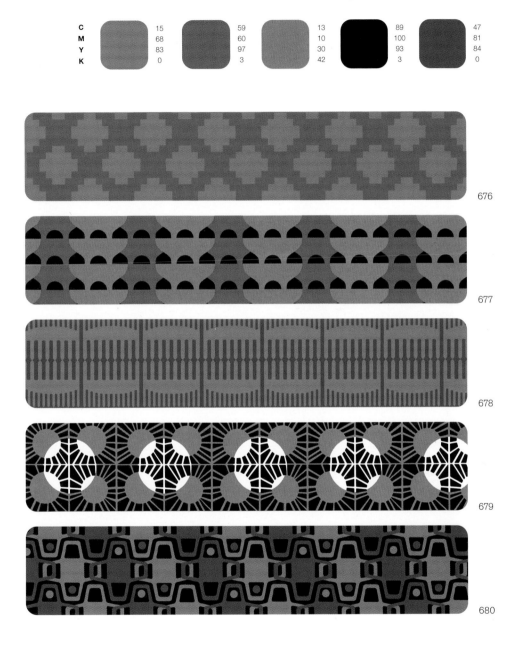

C	15		59		13		89		47
M	68		60		10		100		81
Y	83		97		30		93		84
K	0		3		42		3		0

676

677

678

679

680

C	37	17	21	0
M	41	30	17	14
Y	97	77	100	50
K	3	3	3	0

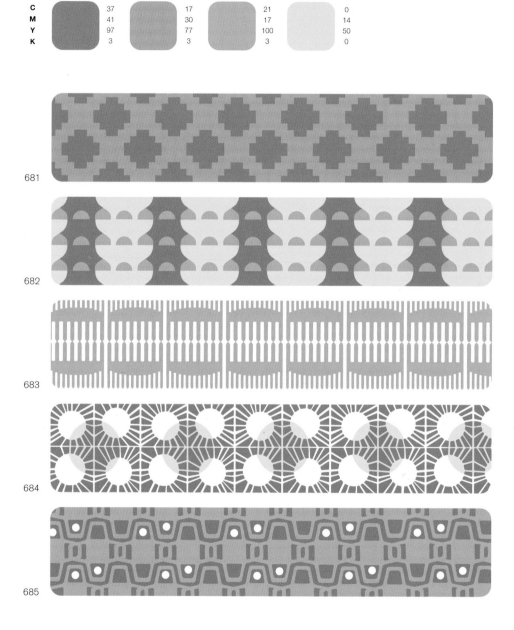

681

682

683

684

685

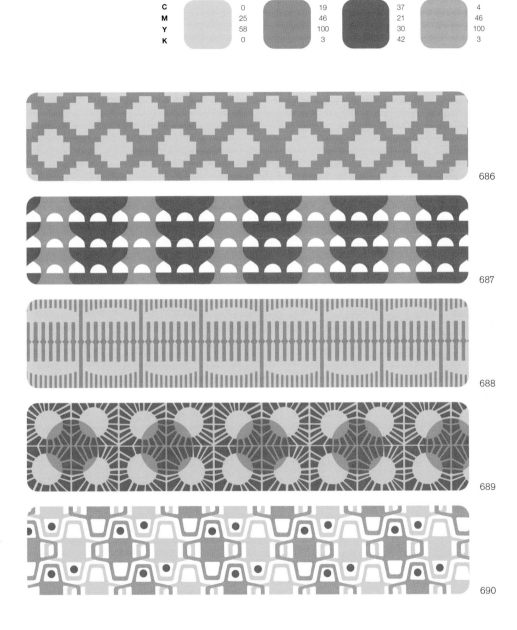

		0		19		37		4
C		0		19		37		4
M		25		46		21		46
Y		58		100		30		100
K		0		3		42		3

686

687

688

689

690

C	5	25	71	26
M	0	26	88	7
Y	90	90	81	11
K	0	0	3	42

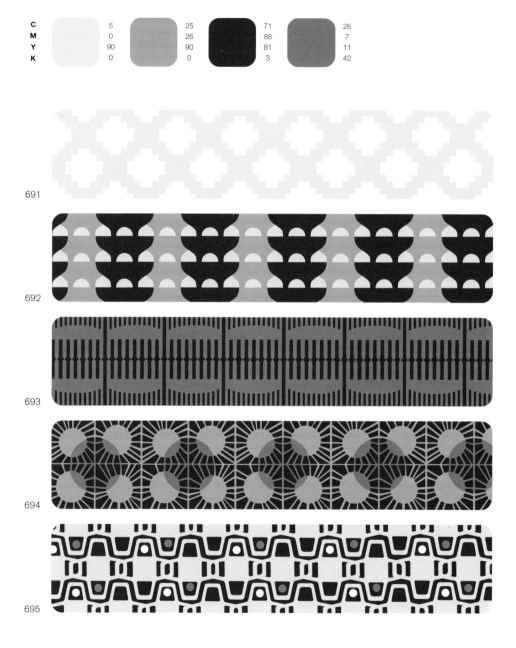

691

692

693

694

695

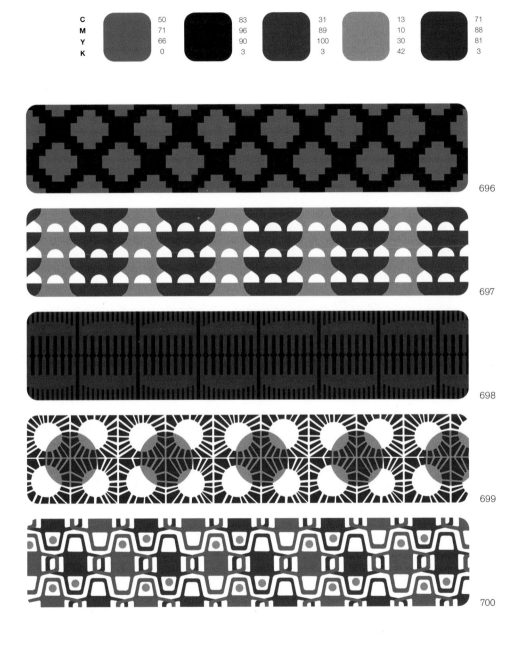

C		50		83		31		13		71
M		71		96		89		10		88
Y		66		90		100		30		81
K		0		3		3		42		3

696

697

698

699

700

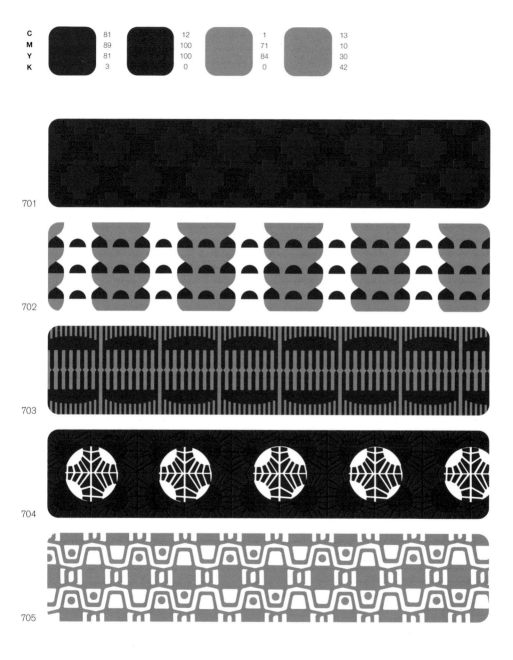

C	81	12	1	13
M	89	100	71	10
Y	81	100	84	30
K	3	0	0	42

701

702

703

704

705

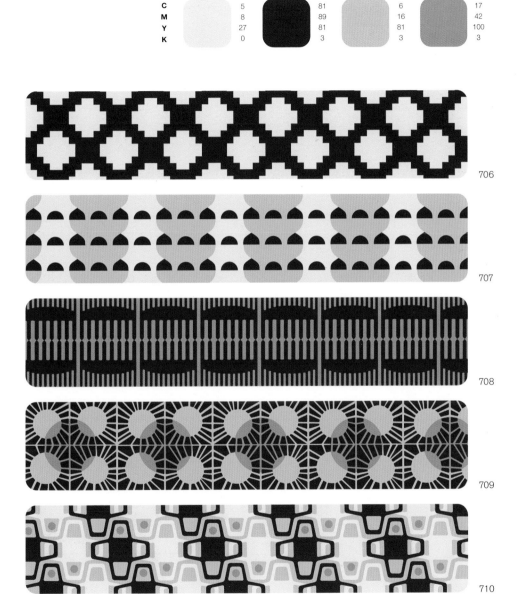

C	5		81		6		17
M	8		89		16		42
Y	27		81		81		100
K	0		3		3		3

706

707

708

709

710

C		13		95		51		59
M		10		100		75		60
Y		30		100		75		97
K		42		3		3		3

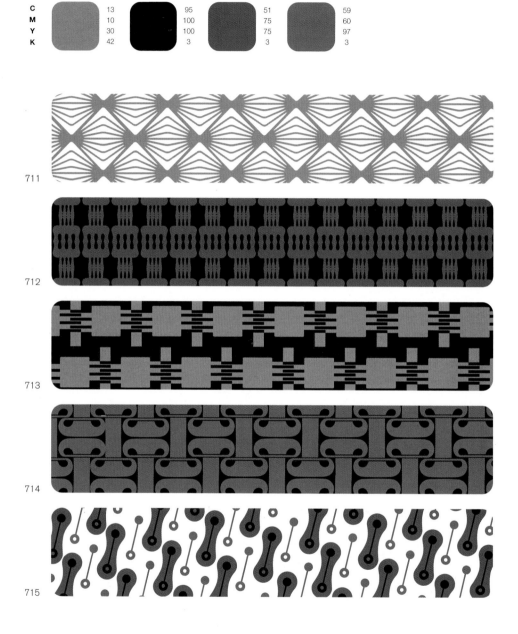

711

712

713

714

715

C	4	13	47	71
M	46	7	69	88
Y	100	12	100	81
K	3	42	0	3

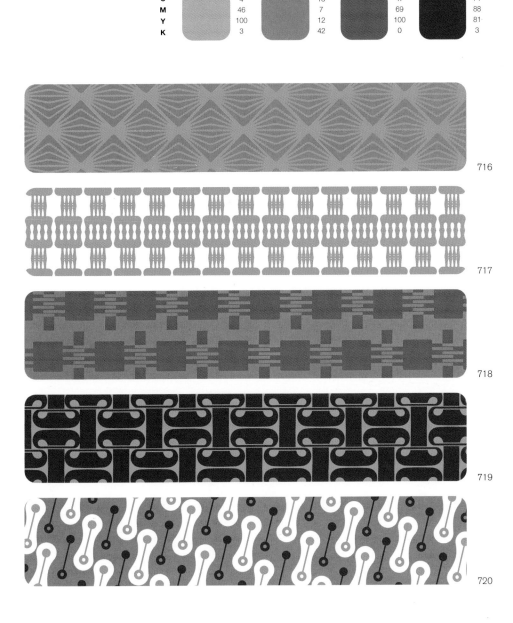

716

717

718

719

720

C	65	88	22	65	13
M	59	100	74	72	7
Y	65	100	83	65	12
K	3	3	0	3	42

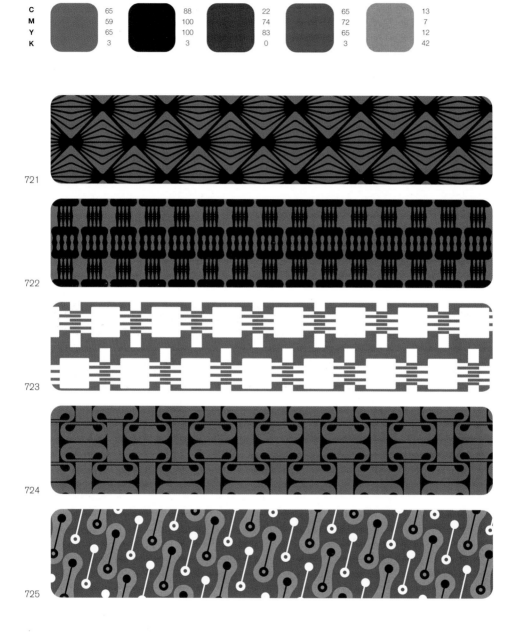

721

722

723

724

725

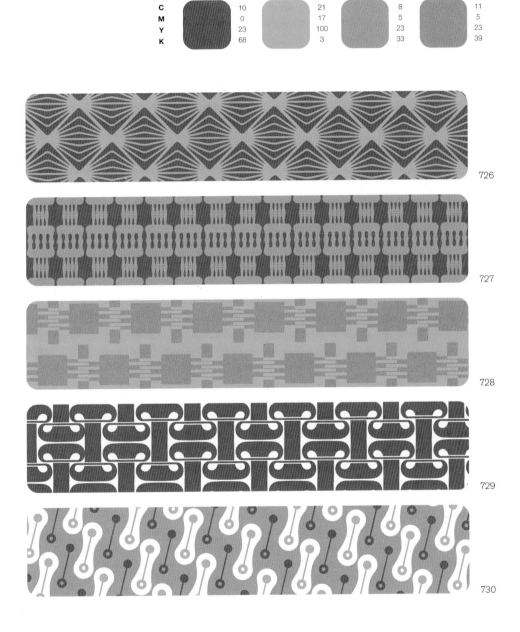

C	10	21	8	11
M	0	17	5	5
Y	23	100	23	23
K	68	3	33	39

726

727

728

729

730

C	45		22		22		0		31
M	47		74		89		39		51
Y	97		83		100		52		52
K	3		42		3		0		0

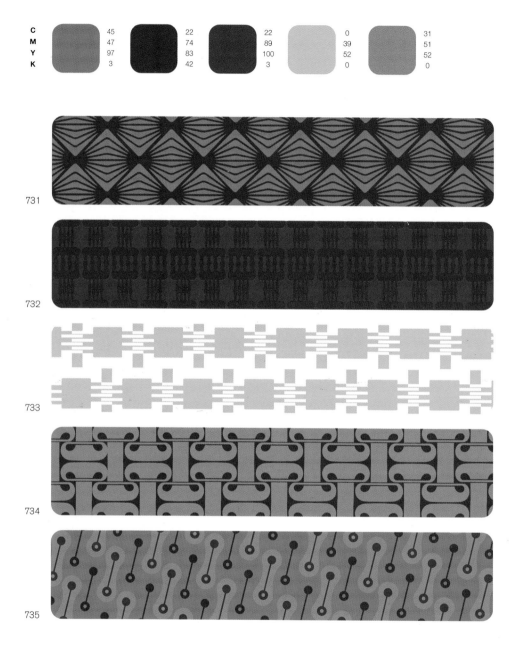

731

732

733

734

735

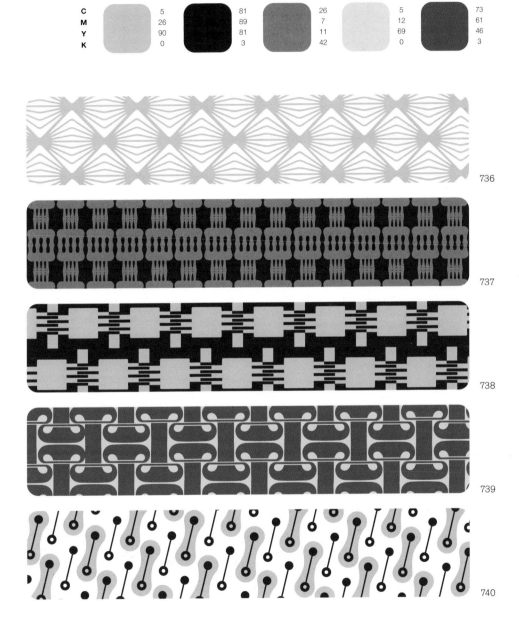

C	5		81		26		5		73
M	26		89		7		12		61
Y	90		81		11		69		46
K	0		3		42		0		3

736

737

738

739

740

C	4	71	37	13
M	46	60	41	10
Y	100	81	97	30
K	0	3	3	42

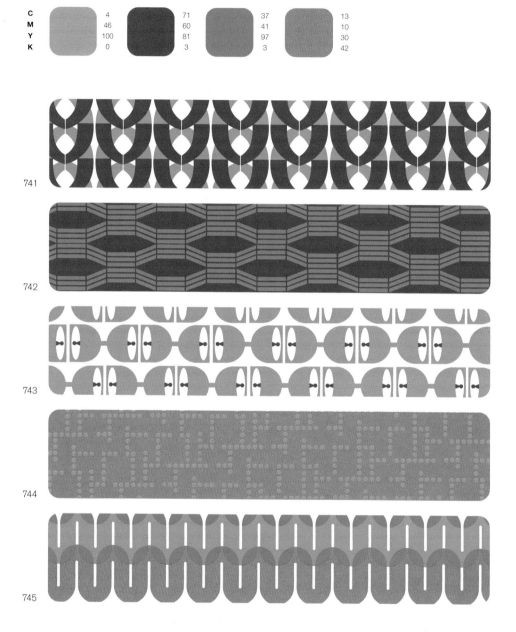

741

742

743

744

745

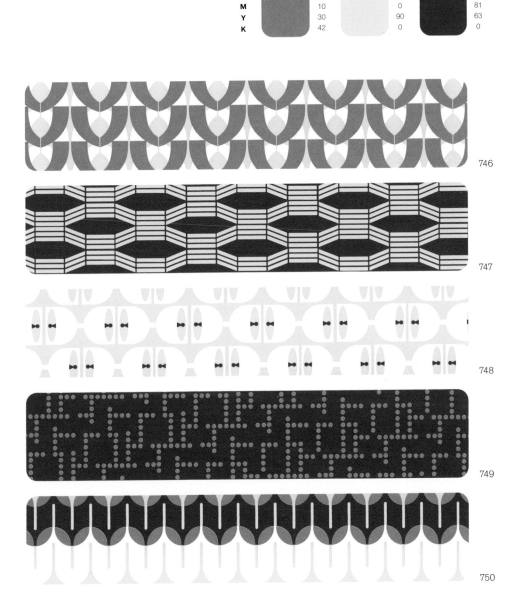

C	13	5	58
M	10	0	81
Y	30	90	63
K	42	0	0

746

747

748

749

750

C 4	31	13	59
M 30	51	10	60
Y 77	52	30	97
K 3	0	42	3

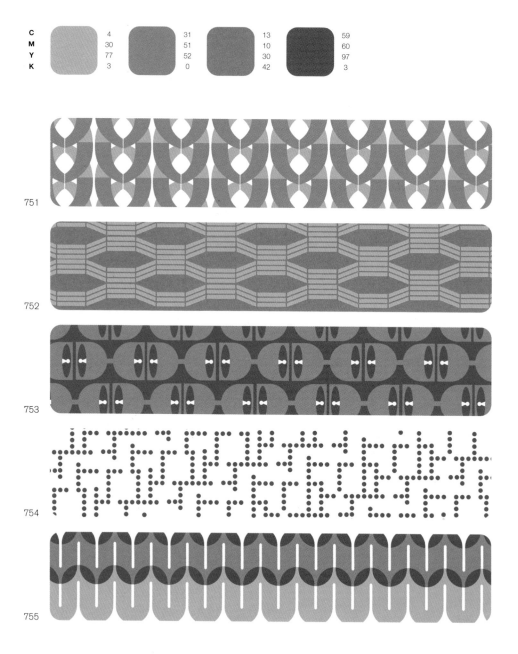

751

752

753

754

755

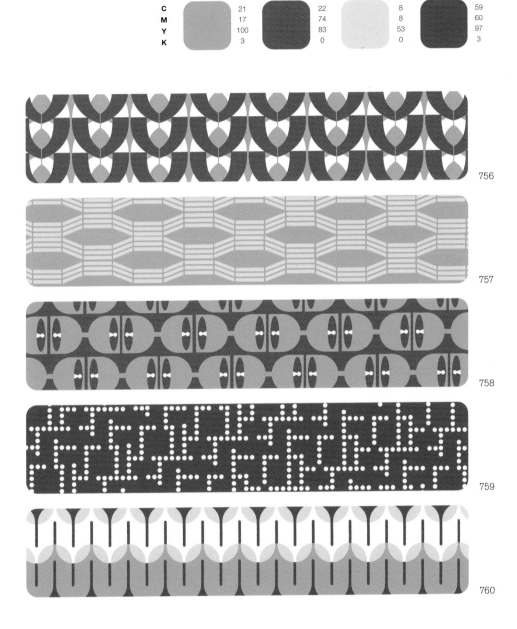

C	21	22	8	59
M	17	74	8	60
Y	100	83	53	97
K	3	0	0	3

756

757

758

759

760

C		5		26		74		21
M		8		7		100		50
Y		27		11		65		100
K		0		42		34		3

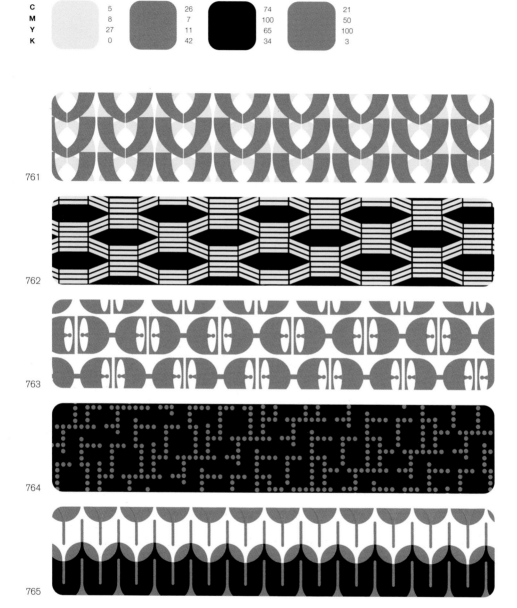

761

762

763

764

765

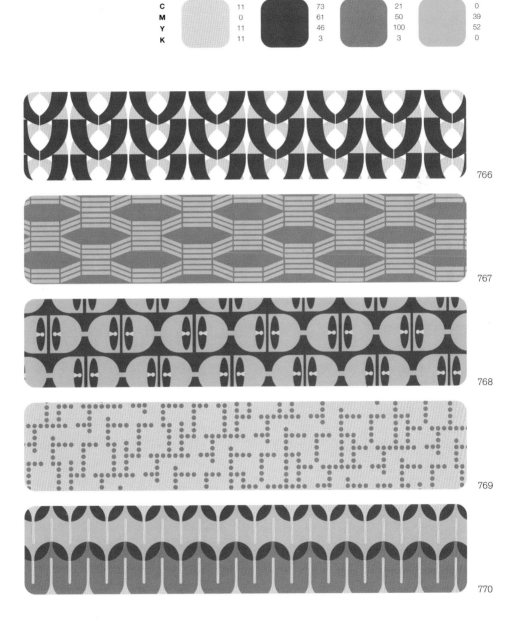

C	11	73	21	0
M	0	61	50	39
Y	11	46	100	52
K	11	3	3	0

766

767

768

769

770

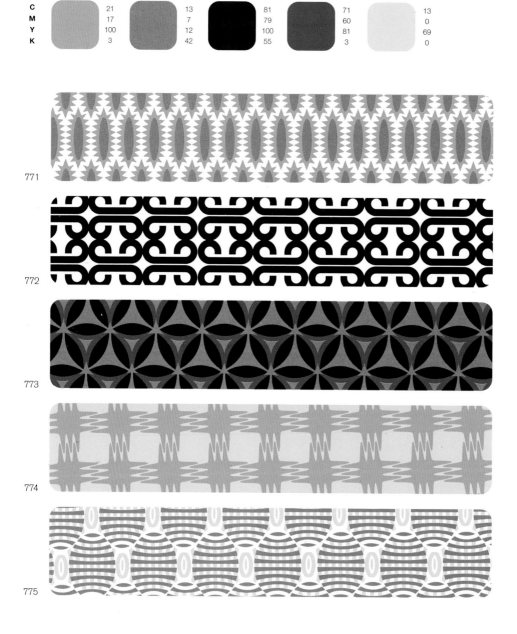

C	21	13	81	71	13
M	17	7	79	60	0
Y	100	12	100	81	69
K	3	42	55	3	0

771

772

773

774

775

C	73	0	74	26	0
M	61	100	100	7	0
Y	46	100	65	11	0
K	3	0	34	42	29

776

777

778

779

780

C	58		91		44		71		88
M	81		100		37		60		100
Y	63		100		97		81		100
K	0		13		3		3		3

781

782

783

784

785

C	15		62		36		26
M	74		91		68		0
Y	83		92		80		0
K	0		3		14		42

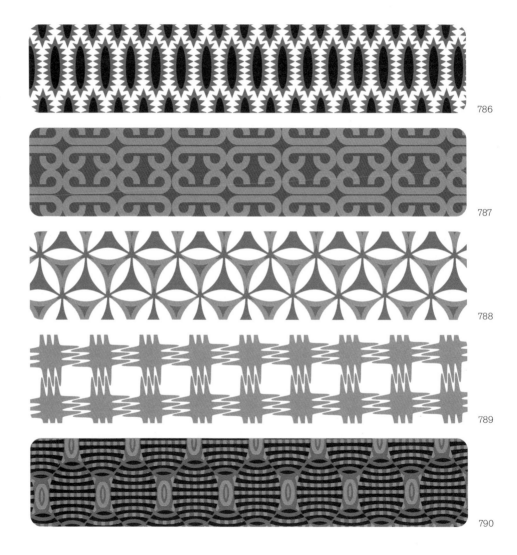

786

787

788

789

790

C		0		50		13		82		4
M		22		67		10		100		46
Y		41		81		30		100		100
K		0		3		42		3		3

791

792

793

794

795

	C	M	Y	K		C	M	Y	K		C	M	Y	K		C	M	Y	K

796

797

798

799

800

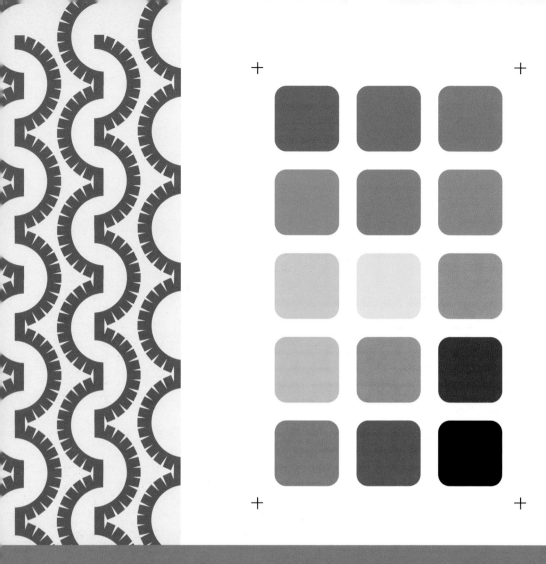

This group of designs pays homage to the ocean—master of pattern, light, and color—and to the nautical world. They take up the challenge of giving form to what is essentially formless and ever-shifting using simple visual gestures and a palette that explores the depths and shallows of the seascape.

Maritime

C	90	65	72	52	65
M	46	62	27	24	24
Y	32	14	89	88	59
K	56	0	53	0	0

801

802

803

804

805

C	18		78		65		2		45
M	50		80		24		46		26
Y	100		81		59		43		41
K	0		51		0		0		0

806

807

808

809

810

	C	M	Y	K
	0	50	45	45	72
	0	44	7	7	8
	0	59	61	91	59
	100	0	75	22	0

811

812

813

814

815

C	13		87		53		83
M	1		100		47		82
Y	66		60		0		5
K	0		0		0		0

816

817

818

819

820

C	38		39		78		0	
M	50		33		35		40	
Y	100		36		32		67	
K	0		0		56		0	

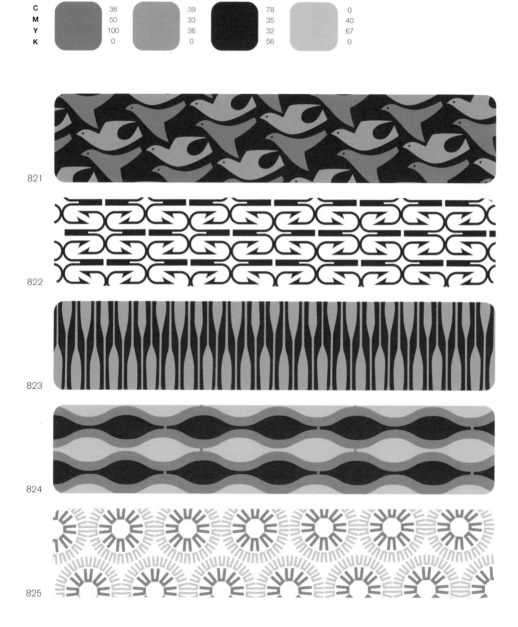

821

822

823

824

825

C	68		78		0		0
M	23		35		70		70
Y	45		32		100		100
K	0		56		23		50

826

827

828

829

830

C	88		16		32		0
M	76		9		31		0
Y	47		90		17		8
K	30		0		0		6

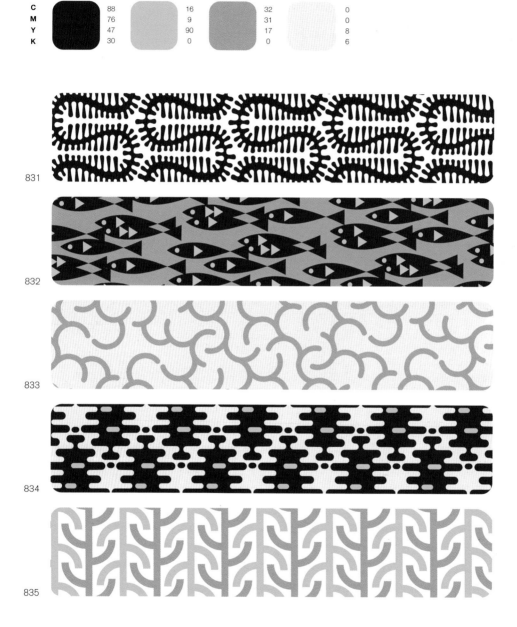

831

832

833

834

835

C	70	91	28	52
M	87	21	35	69
Y	79	15	85	55
K	0	0	0	0

836

837

838

839

840

C	54	68	87	100	38
M	0	73	86	31	37
Y	49	100	79	50	100
K	0	0	0	0	0

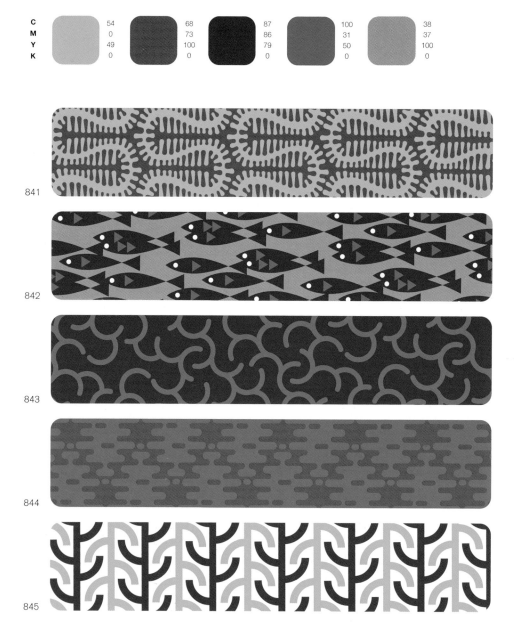

841

842

843

844

845

C	74		56		63		75
M	89		65		50		100
Y	67		9		100		92
K	0		0		0		0

846

847

848

849

850

C	0	97	56	77	0
M	61	94	55	44	14
Y	90	90	51	30	22
K	0	0	0	0	0

851

852

853

854

855

C	68		69		41		11
M	73		6		30		0
Y	100		38		62		15
K	0		0		0		0

856

857

858

859

860

C		88		23		64		20		59
M		75		60		27		27		54
Y		100		50		66		100		100
K		0		5		0		0		5

861

862

863

864

865

C	78		55		2		25
M	41		60		35		5
Y	47		65		100		24
K	0		40		0		0

866

867

868

869

870

C	36	80	24	70
M	35	35	84	64
Y	100	10	97	49
K	0	0	7	0

871

872

873

874

875

C	52	54	54	6	91
M	24	0	37	21	93
Y	88	49	65	16	100
K	0	0	0	0	0

876

877

878

879

880

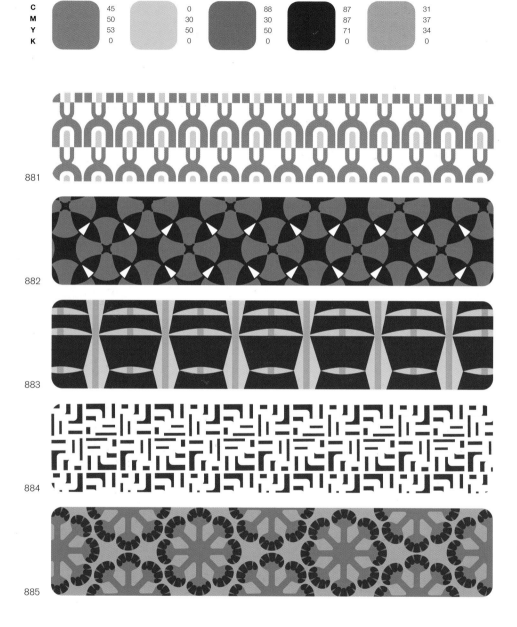

C	45	0	88	87	31
M	50	30	30	87	37
Y	53	50	50	71	34
K	0	0	0	0	0

881

882

883

884

885

C	0	79	37	54	71
M	54	22	47	0	64
Y	71	75	100	49	70
K	0	0	0	0	5

891

892

893

894

895

C	88	33	56
M	95	13	80
Y	47	100	50
K	30	0	0

896

897

898

899

900

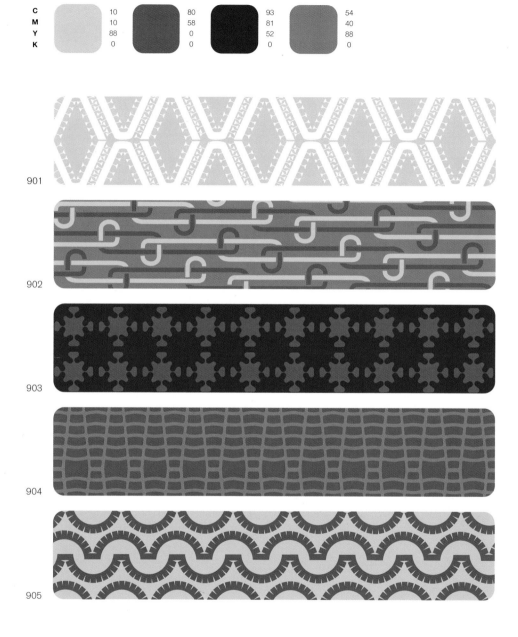

C	10	80	93	54
M	10	58	81	40
Y	88	0	52	88
K	0	0	0	0

901

902

903

904

905

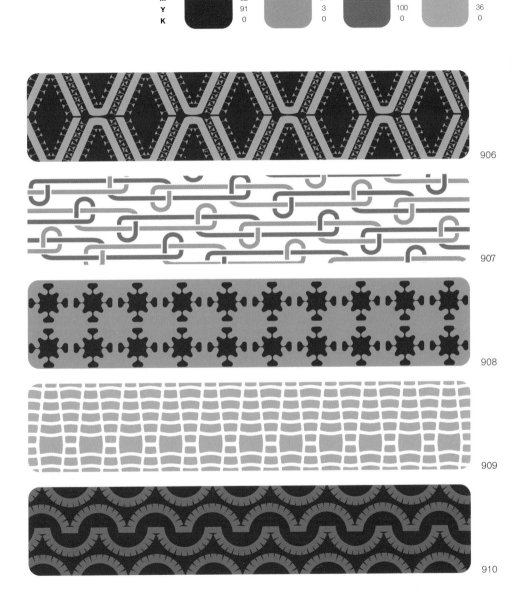

C	81	54	37	33
M	82	27	64	28
Y	91	3	100	36
K	0	0	0	0

906

907

908

909

910

C	50	2	78
M	0	48	56
Y	33	72	100
K	0	0	0

911

912

913

914

915

C	68		80		80		80		97
M	52		0		66		15		92
Y	88		23		88		29		80
K	0		0		88		15		0

916

917

918

919

920

C	79	7	93	27
M	53	4	93	32
Y	22	11	70	24
K	0	0	5	0

921

922

923

924

925

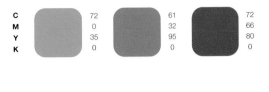

C	72
M	0
Y	35
K	0

61
32
95
0

72
66
80
0

926

927

928

929

930

C	50		91		45
M	93		30		20
Y	12		69		0
K	31		0		0

931

932

933

934

935

C	18	52	71
M	17	89	32
Y	22	94	37
K	0	0	0

936

937

938

939

940

C	59		22		90		59
M	61		3		88		56
Y	65		100		82		100
K	5		0		0		0

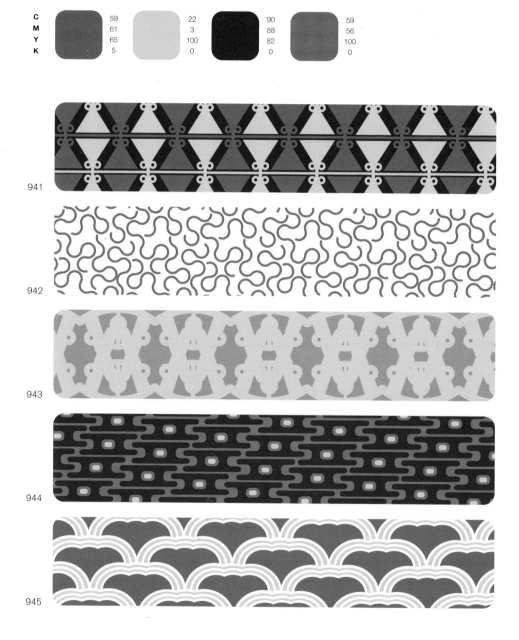

941

942

943

944

945

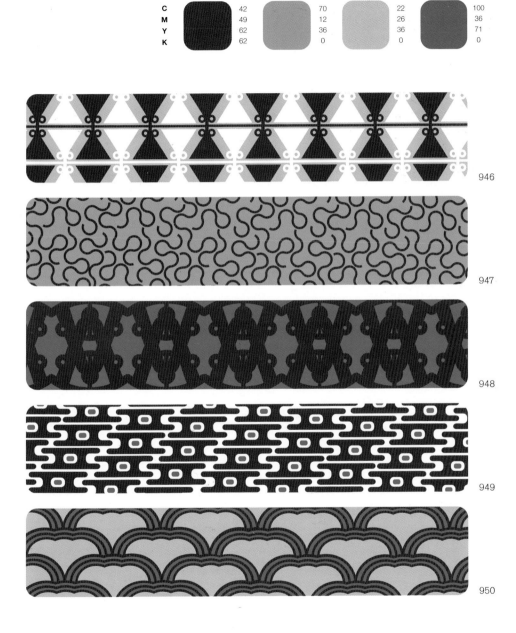

C	42		70		22		100
M	49		12		26		36
Y	62		36		36		71
K	62		0		0		0

946

947

948

949

950

About the Author

Gillian Blease is a freelance illustrator based in London. She studied fine art at university and worked as an artist for a number of years until an introduction to computer graphics led to a change of direction and a new world of briefs and deadlines. Clients include The British Council, Random House Publishing, and BBC Worldwide. She is a regular contributor to the *The Guardian* newspaper. Over the past couple of years Blease has begun to explore her love of pattern design (regarding it as the perfect combination of discipline and freedom) and considers this strand in her career an antidote to the current affairs and contemporary issues she illustrates on a daily basis. www.gillianblease.co.uk